W9-BCD-565

YOSEMITE
• THE COMPLETE GUIDE •

JAMES KAISER

CONTENTS

ADVENTURES (P.19–31)

Hiking, backpacking, rock climbing, river rafting, winter sports—Yosemite has it all!

BASICS (P.32)

Essential Yosemite info, from lodging and camping to weather and black bears.

GEOLOGY (P.41)

Learn about the powerful forces that shaped Yosemite over millions of years, including ancient volcanoes and Ice Age glaciers.

ECOLOGY & WILDLIFE (P.57)

Covering 10,000 feet of mountainous elevation, Yosemite is home to thousands of fascinating plants and animals that coexist in remarkable ways.

HISTORY (P.89)

Yosemite was first settled by the Ahwahneechee Indians. Following the Gold Rush, adventurous tourists and artists discovered its charms. The park later inspired visionaries such as John Muir and Ansel Adams, and in the mid-20th century Yosemite's cliffs gave birth to the modern sport of Big Wall rock climbing.

YOSEMITE VALLEY (P.127)

The most famous part of the park, home to 2,000-foot waterfalls, soaring cliffs, and towering granite domes.

GLACIER POINT ROAD (P.189)

Perched on the edge of Yosemite Valley's south rim, Glacier Point offers a sweeping panorama 3,000 feet above the Valley floor.

TIOGA ROAD (P.215)

This 46-mile road takes you deep into the heart of the High Sierra—a gorgeous alpine wilderness filled with shimmering lakes, snow-capped peaks, and some of the best scenery in the park.

TUOLUMNE MEADOWS (P.241)

Kick back in the Sierra Nevada's largest subalpine meadow and escape the summer crowds. Tuolumne Meadows is the starting point for many of Yosemite's best hikes.

WAWONA & HETCH HETCHY (P.287, 293)

Wawona is home to the Mariposa Grove of giant sequoias, the largest grove in the park. Hetch Hetchy—once a beautiful valley; now a flooded reservoir—inspired one of America's earliest environmental battles.

YOSEMITE
THE COMPLETE GUIDE

Written & Photographed
by James Kaiser

This book would not have been possible without the help of many generous people. Special thanks to Beth Pratt, Kenny Karst, Pete Divine, Bob Fry, Greg Stock, Greg Cox, Linda Eade, Chris Stein, Paul Rogers, Jean Redle, Josia Lamberto-Egan, Peter Bohler, Peter Brewitt, YA, DNC, the entire staff at YNP, and everyone who spent time with me in the wilderness. Above all, special thanks to superstar ranger Dick Ewart, whose wisdom, kindness, and sense of humor have inspired thousands of visitors, including me.

As always, a very special thanks to my family, friends, and all the wonderful people I encountered while working on this guide.

All information in this guide has been exhaustively researched, but names, phone numbers, and other details do change. If you encounter a change or mistake while using this guide, please send an email to changes@jameskaiser.com. Your input will help make future editions of this guide even better.

Although every attempt has been made to ensure the accuracy of information contained within this guide, the author and publisher do not assume and disclaim any liability to any party for any loss or damage caused by errors or omissions. Information has been obtained from sources believed to be reliable, but its accuracy and completeness are not guaranteed. If the rigors and threats of nature are in any way beyond your capabilities, do not attempt any hike in this guide. Many photos contained within this guide depict people in precarious situations; do not assume that any situations depicted in this book are in any way safe. All maps in this guide are based on official USGS data, but serious hikers should supplement their outings with detailed hiking maps.

Additional Photography & Image Credits
Getty Images: page 4, 24, 141
National Park Service: page 51, 89, 90, 91, 92, 93, 99, 101,
102, 106, 109, 110, 114, 117, 157, 195, 291
North Wind Picture Archives: page 94, 97, 100, 107, 111
Wildlife Stock Photos: page 72, 73, 76, 78, 79, 80, 82, 83
Peter Bohler: page 23, 230

FROM THE AUTHOR

THIS BOOK SHOWS you the best that Yosemite has to offer. From lazy strolls in Yosemite Valley to multiday backpacks in the High Sierra, it gives you everything you need to know to make the most of your time in the park. Yosemite is huge, roughly 1,200 square miles, and its size can be overwhelming—especially for first-time visitors. This book breaks it down geographically, exploring the most spectacular regions in detail and skimming over the park's less interesting sights.

If you're a first-time visitor, this book covers all the basics—lodging, camping, transportation, etc. If you've been here before, this book offers a wealth of additional, in-depth information. Over 20 hikes are featured, showcasing some of the park's most remote and rugged regions, and detailed chapters on geology, ecology, and history reveal the fascinating story behind the scenery.

Writing and photographing this book has been an amazing experience. When I first started working on *Yosemite: The Complete Guide*, I figured it would take one year to complete. It took three. There was so much to see, so much that changed from season to season, that one year, I soon realized, could never do Yosemite justice. For three years I explored every aspect of the park. I photographed waterfalls in the spring, backpacked the High Sierra in the summer, and went cross country skiing in the winter. During my travels I became friends with some of the park's most legendary rangers and employees, each of whom imparted their love and knowledge of Yosemite to me. It's my goal to pass that love and knowledge on to you.

Happy trails,

INTRODUCTION

NESTLED DEEP IN the heart of the Sierra Nevada Mountains, Yosemite is considered by many to be America's finest national park. Its luminous granite is bursting with superlatives: the highest waterfall in North America (Yosemite Falls), the most famous vertical rock face in the world (El Capitan), and the largest organisms of all time (giant sequoias). But no statistic can ever capture the park's staggering beauty. Yosemite has inspired some of America's finest artists, and its remarkable scenery continues to lure millions of visitors each year.

Yosemite Valley is the crown jewel of the park. Just seven miles long by one mile wide, it represents less than 1% of the park's 1,200 square miles. But concentrated among the Valley's forests, meadows, and 3,000-foot cliffs are some of the world's most remarkable natural features—Half Dome, El Capitan, Yosemite Falls. Because Yosemite Valley is the most popular part of the park, it's home to the vast majority of Yosemite's lodges, campgrounds, and visitor facilities.

Above Yosemite Valley lies the High Sierra: a stunning alpine wilderness of shimmering lakes, snow-capped peaks, and oceans of sparkling granite. Reached via Tioga Road—the only road that bisects the park—the High Sierra is an outdoor paradise for hikers, backpackers, and rock climbers. Tuolumne Meadows, lying at an elevation of 8,600 feet, is the High Sierra's unofficial headquarters—the starting point for many spectacular hikes.

The park's southern tip is home to Wawona, famous for its proximity to the Mariposa Grove of giant sequoias (the largest of the park's three sequoia groves). Twenty miles north of Yosemite Valley lies Hetch Hetchy—once a beautiful valley, now a massive reservoir. Although its waterfalls are impressive in the spring, Hetch Hetchy is interesting mainly for the contentious environmental battles it spawned nearly a century ago.

Yosemite Valley was first settled by the Ahwahneechee Indians. Following the Gold Rush, adventurous artists sought out the remote mountain valley, and their dramatic paintings and photographs made Yosemite internationally famous. John Muir arrived in 1868, and his writings helped spur the creation of Yosemite National Park in 1890. In 1916 Ansel Adams made his first trip to the park. Then, starting in the 1930s, rock climbers pioneered advanced techniques in Yosemite that are now used throughout the world. Today Yosemite's cliffs, peaks, and waterfalls lure over four million visitors a year.

Left: Descending Half Dome's cables

Pohono Trail

Tenaya Lake

Half Dome

Mariposa Grove of Giant Sequoias

Bachelor and
Three Graces

HIKING & BACKPACKING

Yosemite OFFERS SOME of the best hiking in the Sierra Nevada—which offers some of the best hiking in America. Over 800 miles of trails crisscross the park, ranging from easy day hikes to rugged multi-day backpacks. There are trails on the floor of Yosemite Valley, trails that skirt the Valley's rim, and trails that explore Yosemite's High Sierra, the spectacular wilderness lying above 8,000 feet. Lush meadows? Glacial lakes? Thirteen thousand-foot peaks? Check, check and check. The only question is where *not* to hike.

Yosemite's hiking season gears up in the spring, when the Sierra Nevada's heavy winter snowpack starts to melt. As the months progress, the snowline creeps higher and higher, and by mid-July most of the park's trails are usually open. But conditions vary considerably from year to year. Following particularly heavy winters, Yosemite's highest trails can stay buried until late July. Always check current conditions before hitting the trail. Yosemite's official website (www.nps.gov/yose) lists current trail conditions, and more detailed info can be gleaned from the experts at Yosemite's Wilderness Centers.

Hiking in the spring and the early summer can be great—waterfalls and wildflowers abound!—but those months are also prime season for mosquitoes. The good news? Mosquito swarms are generally limited to the three weeks following snowmelt. But mosquito numbers, like snowfall, vary considerably from year to year; some years they're bad, some years they're not. Ask about mosquito conditions if you visit in May, June or July, and always bring plenty of bug repellent.

July and August are the most popular hiking months. Other than the occasional afternoon thundershower, days are sunny and dry, and nights are clear under an ocean of stars. September is one of the best months for hiking—the crowds have thinned out and the days are sunny and mild—but temperatures at high elevations generally start plunging by the end of the month. The first big snowfall usually hits by mid-November, at which point Tioga Road and Tuolumne Meadows—the popular gateways to the High Sierra—shut down.

Day hikers can explore any trail whenever they like. Backpackers, however, must obtain permits to spend the night in the wilderness. Serious hikers and backpackers should also purchase a detailed topographic map. My personal favorite is National Geographic's Trails Illustrated, which shows day-use areas, campfire boundaries, and a wealth of other useful information.

Left: The Clark Range

HIKING BASICS

- Stay on the trail.
- Carry and drink plenty of water, and wear UV protection.
- Pets and bicycles are only allowed on paved trails.
- Horses and mules have the right of way.
- Pack out what you pack in.

WILDERNESS PERMITS

Wilderness permits are required for all overnight backpacks in the park. The permits, issued by the Yosemite Association, can be reserved in advance or picked up on the day of (or the day before) the start of your backpack at one of the park's five Wilderness Centers. Daily limits are placed on the number of permits issued for each trailhead (60% of permits for a given trailhead can be reserved up to 24 weeks in advance; the remaining 40% are available starting 24 hours before your trip on a first-come, first-served basis). The system, while sometimes frustrating, is designed to reduce overcrowding in the wilderness. Once you have a permit in hand, it's great. By limiting the number of overnight hikers, the park ensures that there are plenty of camping spots and a reasonable amount of solitude on the trail.

When applying for a permit, you'll need the following information: your entry trailhead, your exit trailhead, the dates of your trip, the number of people in your party, and your destination. Advance reservations are available by phone (209-372-0740), by mail (Yosemite Association, PO Box 545, Yosemite, CA 95389), or online (www.nps.gov/yose/wilderness). There is a $5 per person fee for all permits reserved in advance. Current trailhead availability is posted online. If you plan to pick up a permit on the day of (or day before) your backpack, arrive at the Wilderness Center as early as possible to beat the rush; during peak season lines can form before opening hours.

WILDERNESS CENTERS

There are five Wilderness Centers in Yosemite. Seasonal hours vary (check *Yosemite Toady* for exact hours of operation or call 209-372-0200). A winter Wilderness Center at Badger Pass is open seasonally.

- Yosemite Valley: located in Yosemite Village
- Tuolumne Meadows: located on the turnoff to Tuolumne Lodge
- Big Oak Flat Road: located at the park's entrance station (Hwy 120)
- Wawona: located at Hill's Studio next to the Wawona Hotel
- Hetch Hetchy: located at the Hetch Hetchy Entrance Station

WEATHER CONCERNS

Summers in the Sierra Nevada are exceptionally sunny and dry, but anything can—and does—happen. In the summer, the biggest concern is afternoon thundershowers, which build with alarming speed when monsoonal systems occasionally pass over the mountains from the east. Do not attempt any exposed hike (Half Dome, Clouds Rest, etc.) if you see dark clouds in the sky. Also be aware that snow can fall at high elevations during any month of the year. Although snow is very rare in the summer, it is possible, so be prepared. No matter when you hike, bring warm clothes and rain gear.

GUIDED HIKES & BACKPACKS

If Yosemite's myriad trails seem a bit intimidating to you, consider spending some money on a guided hike. Two outstanding organizations offer guided hikes and overnight backpacks in the park, and many of the trips are led by Yosemite experts who will point out fascinating plants, animals, and geologic formations on the trail. The **Yosemite Association** (www.yosemite.org, 209-379-2321) offers guided day hikes and overnight backpacks with an emphasis on outdoor education. They offer a wide range of outdoor seminars throughout the year. **Delaware North** (www.yosemitepark.com, 209-372-8344) also offers guided dayhikes, as well as overnight backpacks with tents, sleeping bags, and other camping equipment provided.

BACKPACKING RULES

WATER
Purify all drinking water using a giardia-rated filter, an iodine based chemical purifier, or by boiling 3–5 minutes.

CAMPFIRES
All campfires are prohibited above 9,600 feet. If you choose to build a campfire, use a previously impacted fire ring and use only dead and fallen wood.

CAMPSITES
Backcountry camping is prohibited within four miles of Yosemite Valley, Glacier Point, Tuolumne Meadows, Wawona, and Hetch Hetchy. Backcountry camping is also prohibited within one mile of any road and within 100 feet of water. Whenever possible, campsites should be at least 100 feet from the trail.

FOOD STORAGE
Overnight hikers must store their food in bear canisters (see below). Metal bear boxes are provided at most trailheads for any food you choose to leave behind.

SOAP & TOOTHPASTE
Never use soaps (even "biodegradable" ones) or toothpaste in any lake, river, or stream. Use soap and toothpaste at least 100 feet away from any water source.

HUMAN WASTE
Bury all human waste in a hole six inches deep at least 100 feet from waters sources. Pack out all toilet paper.

BEAR CANISTERS

Although generally harmless if undisturbed, black bears in Yosemite are notorious for attempting to raid backpackers' food. As a result, there are steps that all wilderness visitors must take to (a) protect their food and (b) help train the bears not to rely on the bounty of backpackers.

For years backpackers were told to place their food in a bag, tie the bag to a rope, and hang the bag from a tall branch at night. At first, it worked. Then the bears started climbing onto the branches. These days the bag-and-rope system has been abandoned in favor of new, high-tech "bear canisters" that can hold up to a week's worth of food for one hiker. You can purchase bear canisters at outdoor stores throughout California or rent them from Yosemite's Wilderness Centers for $5. Lock all food and scented items (toothpaste, soap, etc.) in your bear canister and place it at least 30 feet from your tent at night. Before going to bed, double check that all food has been removed from your tent.

YOSEMITE'S BEST HIKES

YOSEMITE VALLEY

The Mist Trail........................166

Half Dome............................172

Four Mile Trail......................178

Yosemite Falls.......................180

The Mist Trail

GLACIER POINT ROAD

Taft Point.............................198

Sentinel Dome......................200

Pohono Trail.........................202

The Clark Range....................206

The Clark Range

TIOGA ROAD

North Dome..........................224

May Lake High Sierra Camp.......228

Clouds Rest..........................230

Sunrise High Sierra Camp............234

Ten Lakes............................236

Clouds Rest

TUOLUMNE MEADOWS

Lembert Dome.......................248

Cathedral Lakes.....................250

Elizabeth Lake.......................252

Glen Aulin High Sierra Camp......254

Gaylor Lakes.........................256

Young Lakes.........................258

Mount Dana.........................266

Vogelsang High Sierra Camp........272

Grand Canyon of the Tuolumne...276

Matterhorn Canyon.................280

Rock Climbing

To SAY YOSEMITE is a good place to rock climb is like saying the Vatican is a good place to pray. To rock climbers, Yosemite is a holy mecca. Some of the world's most famous climbs are located in Yosemite Valley, and some of the sport's most innovative techniques and equipment were pioneered here over the past seven decades. Yosemite's vast granite walls attract tens of thousands of climbers each year. Beginners come to learn, great climbers spend years becoming experts, and experts follow in the footsteps—and footholds—of climbing legends.

Rock climbing in Yosemite runs the gamut from easy bouldering (scampering over large boulders) to multi-day, 3,000-foot expeditions where climbers haul up food, water, and supplies, then spend the night strapped to a portable ledge. If a breezy night suspended thousands of feet in the air doesn't inspire your inner Spider Man, there are less intimidating ways to enjoy the sport. The **Yosemite Mountaineering School** offers rock climbing lessons in Yosemite Valley from mid-April through October (www.yosemitepark.com, 209-372-8344). They offer beginner, intermediate, and advanced lessons, as well as two-day seminars on Big Wall Climbing. You can also hire private guides to lead you up the Valley's most storied landmarks, including El Capitan and Half Dome. They supply the equipment and food—you supply the cojones.

Summers are hot in Yosemite Valley (elevation: 4,000 feet), driving many rock climbers to the higher, cooler region around Tuolumne Meadows (elevation: 8,600 feet). In the summer, Yosemite Mountaineering School operates a sister branch in Tuolumne Meadows (209-372-8435) that also offers lessons.

A comprehensive guide to Yosemite rock climbing is beyond the scope of this book. If you're a bona fide rock jock, there are plenty of great climbing guides available in stores throughout the park.

Despite rock climbing's inherent danger, there are relatively few climbing accidents in Yosemite. The key word is *relatively*. There are still, on average, over 100 climbing accidents and 15 climbing parties that require rescue each year. When bad weather or injuries threaten climbers lives, Yosemite Search And Rescue (YOSAR) steps into action. Their world-class team of superhuman climbers scampers up and down vertical walls in harrowing conditions, performing complex rescue operations thousands of feet above the ground. Their exploits are legendary, and their techniques are copied throughout the world.

HIGH SIERRA CAMPS

YOSEMITE'S HIGH SIERRA Camps provide a fantastic way for visitors who enjoy a warm bed, a hot shower, and a hearty meal to experience the beauty of the backcountry. There are five High Sierra Camps sprinkled throughout the park, each with a dining hall, a shower house, and several canvas tent cabins heated by a wood burning stove.

Each High Sierra Camp is located in a beautiful setting, and together they are connected by a 47-mile hiking loop. You can hike to any of the High Sierra Camps in a single day, or hike from camp to camp over several days, spending a night at each one. But due to the immense popularity of the High Sierra Camps, initial reservations are granted by a lottery system in November and December for spots the following summer. You can enter the lottery by phone, mail, or email (visit www.yosemitepark.com or call 559-253-5674 for details). If you miss the lottery or don't get a spot, additional dates become available around mid-May on a first-come, first-served basis, and cancellations sometimes open up spots in the spring and summer. Rates at High Sierra Camps are about $125 per night for adults, $70 per night for children.

Another option is to pay for a multi-day Saddle Trip, riding from camp to camp on a mule, or a multi-day Guided Hike, led by a knowledgeable ranger who points out fascinating natural features as you hike from camp to camp. Saddle trips and Guided Hikes are pricey ($830 for a 4-day Saddle Trip; $1,310 for a 6-day Saddle Trip; $825 for a 5-day Guided Hike; $1,160 for a 7-day Guided Hike), but they're definitely worth it (call 559-253-5674 for reservations).

The High Sierra Camps are generally open from early July to early September. Opening dates can be pushed back, however, following winters with heavy snow. In 2005, a year which saw nearly 200% of average snowfall, the High Sierra Camps did not open at all.

The only High Sierra Camp hike not listed in this book is Merced Lake, which is arguably the least scenic of the five *and* takes many people two days to hike to. Merced Lake is the largest High Sierra Camp, however, which means you can often find space there if the other camps are full. Note: High Sierra Camp tent cabins are communal, which means your bed will be one of several in the tent cabin. Tent cabins are split male/female. Also note that Vogelsang and Glen Aulin do not have showers.

Left: Vogelsang High Sierra Camp

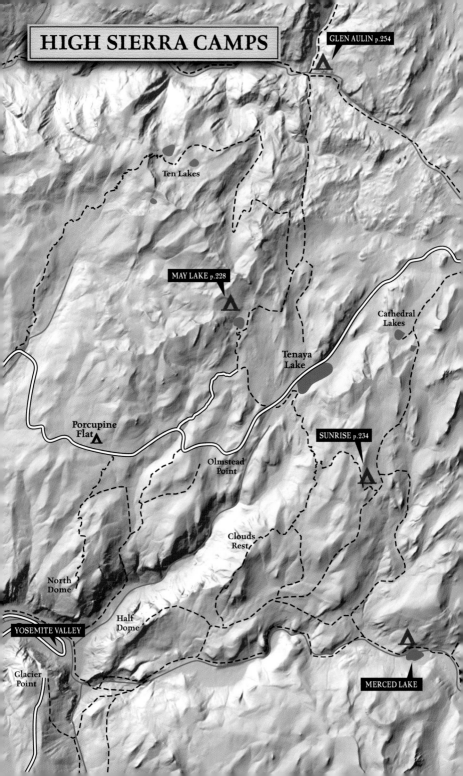

HIGH SIERRA CAMPS

GLEN AULIN p.254

Ten Lakes

MAY LAKE p.228

Cathedral
Lakes

Tenaya
Lake

Porcupine
Flat

SUNRISE p.234

Olmstead
Point

Clouds
Rest

North
Dome

Half
Dome

YOSEMITE VALLEY

Glacier
Point

MERCED LAKE

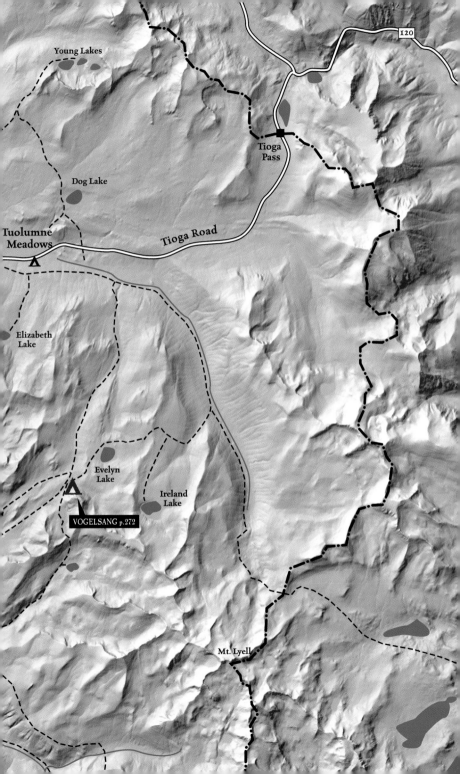

Young Lakes

120

Tioga Pass

Dog Lake

Tuolumne
Meadows

Tioga Road

Elizabeth
Lake

Evelyn
Lake

Ireland
Lake

VOGELSANG p.272

Mt. Lyell

WINTER SPORTS

WHEN PEOPLE THINK Yosemite, they think glorious summer days filled with hiking, rock climbing, and plenty of mountain sunshine. But the Sierra Nevada—the second snowiest range in North America—is also a fantastic winter destination. And while ski resorts like Tahoe and Mammoth capture the headlines, there's plenty of alpine fun to be had in Yosemite.

Badger Pass Ski Resort (p.191) is located about 20 miles from Yosemite Valley along Glacier Point Road. It's not much of a challenge, but Badger Pass is a great beginner's slope with reasonable prices and over 100 miles of XC ski trails.

Yosemite also offers two popular overnight XC ski trips. The most spectacular is the guided 10.5-mile ski trip from Badger Pass to Glacier Point, where you'll spend the night in a cozy hut on the rim of Yosemite Valley. Prices range from $160–$190 for a one-night trip to $240–$290 for a two-night trip; meals included. (209-372-8444, www.yosemitepark.com). The other (more rugged) option is an overnight trip to Ostrander Ski Hut, located on Ostrander Lake nine miles southeast of Badger Pass. This stone building offers 25 beds, cooking facilities, and plenty of rustic charm—all for just $20 per night. Reservations are booked through the Yosemite Association (209-372-0740, www.yosemite.org). Still want more? Call 209-372-8444 and ask about multi-day, High Sierra XC ski tours.

RIVER RAFTING

THE MERCED RIVER, which twists and turns through Yosemite Valley before exiting the park near the town of El Portal, offers two kinds of rafting experiences: mellow and exciting.

Mellow: In the summer, Curry Village rents six-person rafts that you can paddle down the Merced River. You'll pass by spectacular views of Half Dome, Yosemite Falls, and El Capitan as you float three gentle miles to Sentinel Beach, where a shuttle picks you up and takes you back to Curry Village. Raft rentals are available only when the Merced is not flowing too high or too low—a window that generally lasts between late May and July. Cost is about $15 per person.

Exciting: Just after the Merced exits the park it offers dozens of heart-pounding rapids as its twists and turns alongside Highway 140. A handful of commercial rafting outfitters offer guided daytrips in the spring and early summer when the water is running high. Trips last a few hours and cost around $150 per person. The best outfitters include OARS (800-346-6277, www.oars.com), Zephyr (800-431-3636, www.zrafting.com), ARTA (800-323-2782, www.arta.org), and Whitewater Voyages (800-400-7238, www.whitewatervoyages.com). OARS and Zephyr also offer both day and overnight trips on the even wilder Tuolumne River just outside Yosemite below Hetch Hetchy Reservoir.

Yosemite
BASICS

GETTING TO YOSEMITE

Yosemite National Park is located in the central Sierra Nevada Mountains in northern California. By car it's about three hours east of San Francisco and about seven hours northeast of Los Angeles. The closest major airport is San Francisco International Airport.

If you'd rather not drive, Amtrak (800-872-7245, www.amtrak.com) and Greyhound (800-231-2222, www.greyhound.com) offer transportation to the city of Merced. From Merced you can purchase a ticket on a bus operated by YARTS, Yosemite Area Regional Transportation (877-989-2787, www.yarts.com), which runs daily buses from Merced, Mariposa, and Midpines year-round. YARTS also offers service from Mammoth Lake on the eastern side of the Sierra Nevada in the summer.

There are four entrances to Yosemite. The Big Oak Flat Entrance, located on the park's eastern boundary along Highway 120, is the closest entrance to San Francisco. Arch Rock Entrance, located on Highway 140, is the closest entrance to the towns of Merced and Mariposa. South Entrance is located along Highway 41 at the park's southern tip, close to Wawona and the Mariposa Grove of giant sequoias. The final park entrance, Tioga Pass, is located along the park's western boundary on the crest of the Sierra. Tioga Pass is accessible via Highway 120 from the small town of Lee Vining, located along Highway 395.

ENTRANCE FEES

Yosemite National Park's entrance fee is $20 per vehicle or $10 per pedestrian, motorcycle rider, or cyclist. Admission is good for seven days. You can also purchase an annual pass to Yosemite ($40) or the America The Beautiful Pass ($80), which gives you unlimited access to all U.S. national parks and federal recreation lands for one full year.

GETTING AROUND YOSEMITE

The park operates a free shuttle in Yosemite Valley throughout the year. A free shuttle is also offered along Tioga Road between Tioga Pass and Olmstead Point in the summer. Seasonal schedules and shuttle times are listed in *Yosemite Today*.

INFORMATION

"YOSEMITE TODAY"

As soon as you enter the park, pick up a copy of Yosemite Today. This free park publication, available at all entrance stations and visitor centers, offers a wealth of seasonal information, including shuttle schedules, hours of operation for shops and restaurants, sunrise/sunset times, and other park essentials.

VISITOR CENTERS

Ranger-staffed visitor centers are located in Yosemite Valley (p.127), Tuolumne Meadows (p.241), and Wawona (p.287). Small information booths are also located at all park hotels.

GAS

A very quick (and *very* important) note on gas in the park: There is NO GAS in Yosemite Valley. There are only three gas stations in the park, located at Crane Flat, Tuolumne Meadows, and Wawona. Though hardly inexpensive, all three are generally cheaper than gas stations located just outside the park.

WHAT TO DO IN ONE DAY

If you're only in Yosemite for one day, head straight to Yosemite Valley (p.127) and spend your time basking in the park's most spectacular sights. In the morning explore Yosemite Valley on foot, by bike, or by car. In the late morning pick up sandwiches at Degnan's Deli (p.129), then head to the Mist Trail (p.166) and have lunch at the top of Vernal Fall. Take a narrated tram tour (p.129) around Yosemite Valley in the afternoon, then cap off your day with a drive to Glacier Point (p.189) for sunset. (If you want to avoid the sunset crowds at Glacier Point, hike to the top of Sentinel Dome, p.200).

WHAT TO DO IN ONE WEEKEND

Saturday: Explore Yosemite Valley following the itinerary listed above.

Sunday: If you find yourself enthralled by giant sequoias, head to Wawona and visit the Mariposa Grove (p.287). Wander among the trees or buy a ticket for a narrated tram tour (p.291). If you'd rather check out the stunning scenery at the park's higher elevations, drive along Tioga Road (p.215) into the High Sierra. If you're short on time, go only as far as Tenaya Lake (p.223). If you've got time to spare, head to Tuolumne Meadows and hike to the top of Lembert Dome (p.248).

WHEN TO VISIT YOSEMITE

SPRING

Spring is the best time to visit Yosemite. The park is relatively uncrowded, waterfalls are at their peak, and Yosemite Valley is in full bloom. The only downside: Tioga Road (which provides access to Tuolumne Meadows and the High Sierra) is often closed in the early spring due to lingering winter snow.

SUMMER

Summer is Yosemite's most popular season in terms of visitation. At times (Memorial Day, Labor Day, Fourth of July) it can be a bit *too* popular, with long lines and traffic jams in Yosemite Valley. Still, the Sierra Nevada's summer weather is famously glorious, and solitude is generally never more than a hike away. Summer is a fantastic time to explore Tuolumne Meadows and the High Sierra.

FALL

Fall is one of the best times to visit Yosemite. The crowds thin out after Labor Day and temperatures in Yosemite start to cool down. September and October are two of the best months for hiking in Yosemite Valley. Although the waterfalls have slowed to a trickle, the foliage in late fall is gorgeous.

WINTER

Winter is Yosemite's least popular season in terms of visitation, but after a fresh layer of snow the park is spectacular. Although Tioga Road shuts down due to heavy snow, cutting off access to Tuolumne Meadows and the High Sierra, Glacier Point Road is plowed as far as Badger Pass, a small ski resort with downhill and cross country skiing.

BEARS

No other topic generates as much fear and confusion in Yosemite as bears. Grainy videos of bears breaking into cars are played on a constant loop on TV monitors in hotel lobbies, and overnight guests are required to sign forms stating they are Bear Aware. Although bears *can* be problematic in Yosemite, they won't be if you follow a few basic rules.

There are hundreds of hungry black bears in Yosemite. The good news: they're not interested in eating you. The bad news: they are *very* interested in getting their paws on any food or scented items (toothpaste, sunscreen, ect.) that you leave unattended. Proper food storage is required at all times. Store anything with a scent (including canned goods, empty coolers, and dirty dishes) in the metal food lockers located throughout the park. Never leave any food or scented items in your tent or tent cabin, never keep food in a hotel room with any doors or windows open, and never leave food in your car after daylight hours.

Vernal Fall

YOSEMITE LODGING & CAMPING

Yosemite's seven hotels and lodges are all run by Delaware North Corporation (559-253-5635, www.yosemitepark.com). Try to book your room as far in advance as possible, *especially* for the busy summer season. Rooms are much easier to come by off-season, and discount rates are often available mid-week and in the winter months. But no matter what time of the year you visit, never show up at the park without a reservation and expect to get a room—chances are you'll be sorely disappointed.

Yosemite's 13 campgrounds are run by the National Park Service. Roughly half of the campgrounds are first-come, first-served; the rest require advance reservations (877-444-6777, www.recreation.gov). Campsites generally accommodate up to six people. There are also three Backpacker Campgrounds where backpackers with wilderness permits can spend the night before and after their trip without advance reservations. Yosemite's three Backpacker Campgrounds are located in Yosemite Valley, Tuolumne Meadows, and Hetch Hetchy.

LODGING IN YOSEMITE VALLEY

AHWAHNEE HOTEL
This sumptuous lodge (p.162) is the pinnacle of luxury in Yosemite. Many people consider it to be one of the finest lodges in America. The only downside: the price. Rooms start at $400 per night and can go as high as $1,000 per night!

YOSEMITE LODGE AT THE FALLS
The motel-style rooms at Yosemite Lodge can't compete with the luxury of the Ahwahnee, but the prices ($150–$180 per night) are much more reasonable. A few deluxe rooms have views of nearby Yosemite Falls (p.134).

CURRY VILLAGE
This labyrinth collection of canvas tent cabins offers the best budget lodging in Yosemite Valley ($80 per night). Although the simple tent cabins are charming, the paper-thin walls can be a drag if you've got noisy neighbors. If you're looking for peace and quiet, book one of Curry Village's wooden cabins, which are slightly more expensive ($90 per night) but nicer and more private. There are also two deluxe cabins ($210 per night) that each have a working fireplace.

HOUSEKEEPING CAMP
Like Curry Village, Housekeeping Camp offers budget lodging ($75 per night). But while the canvas tent cabins at Curry Village feel rustic and charming, Housekeeping Camp's bunker-style rooms feel stark and bare. Still, nothing can take away from Housekeeping Camp's spectacular location along the banks of the Merced River. A few rooms even have terrific river views.

CAMPING IN YOSEMITE VALLEY

There are four campgrounds in Yosemite Valley, and all are exceedingly popular. The three "Pines" campgrounds, located at the far eastern end of Yosemite Valley, require reservations (877-444-6777, www.recreation.gov). Only Camp 4 (p.138) is first-come, first-served, but long lines often form early in the morning for any campsites that become available. Camping note: Hot showers can be purchased at Curry Village in the afternoon.

UPPER PINES CAMPGROUND
Open year-round, 238 sites, RVs up to 35 feet, $20/night.

LOWER PINES CAMPGROUND
Open March–October (approximately), 60 sites, RVs up to 40 feet, $20/night.

NORTH PINES CAMPGROUND
Open April–September (approximately), 81 sites, RVs up to 40 feet, $20/night.

CAMP 4
Camp 4 (p.138), located just east of Yosemite Falls, is the only first come, first served campground in Yosemite Valley. Open year-round, 35 sites, no RVs, $5 per person/night (a total of six people will be assigned to each campsite).

LODGING IN TUOLUMNE MEADOWS
TUOLUMNE MEADOWS LODGE
Tuolumne Lodge offers 69 canvas tent cabins that are nearly identical to the tent cabins found in Curry Village in Yosemite Valley, but with the added bonus of a wood-burning stove to keep you warm at night. A central shower house provides bathrooms and hot showers.

CAMPING IN TUOLUMNE MEADOWS

There's only one campground in Tuolumne Meadows, but there are a handful of campgrounds between Yosemite Valley Tuolumne Meadows along Tioga Road (see following page). There are also several small campgrounds located in Inyo National Forest just east of Tioga Pass (www.www.fs.fed.us/r5/inyo) Camping note: Hot showers can be purchased at Tuolumne Lodge in the afternoon.

TUOLUMNE MEADOWS CAMPGROUND
This is the largest campground in the park (304 sites). Half of the sites can be reserved in advance; half are available on a first-come, first-served basis. Open July–September (approximately), RVs up to 35 feet, $20/night.

OTHER LODGING IN THE PARK

WHITE WOLF LODGE
White Wolf, located along Tioga Road (p.215), offers stove-heated, canvas tent cabins like those found at Tuolumne Lodge. ($75 per night).

WAWONA HOTEL
This large, historic hotel (p.289) is bursting with Victorian charm. Some rooms have private baths ($195 per night) others do not ($125 per night). Located in Wawona near the park's southern boundary.

OTHER CAMPGROUNDS IN THE PARK

BRIDALVEIL CREEK CAMPGROUND
Located about halfway up Glacier Point Road (p.189). Open July–September (approximately), no reservations, 110 sites, $14/night, RVs up to 35 feet.

CRANE FLAT CAMPGROUND
Located near the junction of Big Oak Flat Road and Tioga Road (p.215) Open July–September (approximately), reservations required, 166 sites, $20/night, RVs up to 27 feet.

HODGDON MEADOW CAMPGROUND
Located near Yosemite's Big Oak Flat Entrance. Open year-round, reservations required, 105 sites, $20/night, RVs up to 35 feet.

TAMARACK FLAT CAMPGROUND
Located off Tioga Road, not too far from Crane Flat. Open late June–September (approximately), no reservations, 52 sites, $10/night, no RVs.

WHITE WOLF CAMPGROUND
Located adjacent to White Wolf Lodge along Tioga Road. Open July–early September (approximately), no reservations, 74 sites, $14/night, RVs up to 27 feet.

YOSEMITE CREEK CAMPGROUND
Located off Tioga Road. Open July–early September (approximately), no reservations, 40 sites, $10/night, no RVs.

PORCUPINE FLAT CAMPGROUND
Located along Tioga Road. Open July–October 15 (approximately), no reservations, 52 sites, $10/night, RVs up to 35 feet.

WAWONA CAMPGROUND
Located in Wawona (p.289). Open year-round, reservations required May–September, 93 sites, $20/night, RVs up to 35 feet.

GATEWAY TOWNS

MARIPOSA, MIDPINES & EL PORTAL

These three towns, located southeast of Yosemite's Arch Rock Entrance along Highway 140, are the closest gateway towns to Yosemite Valley. Mariposa, located about 45 minutes away from the Arch Rock Entrance Station, is a charming small town with a quaint boardwalk-lined Main Street. With about a dozen restaurants, Mariposa is your best bet for dining outside the park. If you don't mind the extra drive, it's also a good bet for a reasonably priced hotel. The tiny towns of Midpines and El Portal consist of a few scattered hotels and restaurants along Highway 140. If you're planning on spending the bulk of your time in Yosemite Valley and every hotel room in the Valley is booked, look for lodging in Mariposa, Midpines, or El Portal.

GROVELAND

Groveland, located along Highway 120 east of the park's Big Oak Flat Entrance, is my favorite gateway town. Though tiny, it's downtown is bursting with Victorian, Gold Rush-era charm. Groveland's most famous institution is the Iron Door Saloon, home to cold drinks, good food, and live entertainment on the weekends. If you're the type of traveler who loves a good Bed & Breakfast, Groveland offers several gems.

FISH CAMP & OAKHURST

Oakhurst, located near the park's southern boundary along Highway 41, is the largest gateway town, filled with minimalls and fast food restaurants. Like Mariposa, it's a good bet for reasonably priced lodging if you don't mind the drive. Just outside the park's southern entrance lies the tiny town of Fish Camp, which is home to a small general store and a handful of charming hotels.

LEE VINING

The tiny town of Lee Vining, located at the eastern base of the Sierra Nevada, revolves almost entirely around Yosemite and Mono Lake tourism. Its main drag along Highway 395 is home to several motels and a handful of restaurants. If you're planning on spending the bulk of your time in Tuolumne Meadows and all of the rooms in Tuolumne Meadows and along Tioga Road are booked, look for lodging in Lee Vining. Note: Tioga Road, which bisects the park and connects Lee Vining to Tuolumne Meadows and Yosemite Valley, closes in the winter due to heavy snow.

For lodging links and additional lodging options outside the park, visit www.jameskaiser.com

GEOLOGY

YOSEMITE IS A dazzling landscape that captivates everyone who sets foot in the park. Stretching from the rolling foothills on the park's western boundary to the jagged 13,000-foot peaks on the Sierra's crest, Yosemite encompasses some of the most dramatic alpine scenery in America.

Even if you know nothing about geology, Yosemite is still an impressive sight. But take the time to learn about the forces that created it, and you'll look upon the park with a fresh set of eyes. What was once amazing will become astounding. What once took your breath away will make your head spin.

On a human timescale Yosemite seems peaceful and serene. On a geological timescale, however, it is violent and exciting. The last glaciers to sweep through the park melted 10,000 years ago. In geological terms, 10,000 years is the blink of an eye. If the age of the Earth (4.5 billion years) was represented by a 24-hour clock, the past 10,000 years would only represent a fraction of the final second before midnight.

The glaciers sculpted graceful valleys, gouged out sheer cliffs, and polished the granite to a shine. They also bulldozed soil and vegetation out of the mountains, scraping the surface clean and creating a frozen landscape nearly devoid of life. The most recent glacial advance started around 50,000 years ago, but at least three distinct periods of glacial advance—and possibly 10 or more—have swept over the Sierra Nevada since the Ice Age began roughly 2.4 million years ago. Each glaciation added a new layer of depth and complexity to Yosemite's landscape, leaving behind thousands of dazzling new features. Today few places in the world offer so many textbook-perfect examples of glacial geology.

Prior to the Ice Age, tectonic forces had thrust up a massive, 400-mile long block of granite that created the Sierra Nevada. As the mountains rose up, ancient rivers raced down their slopes, carving out deep valleys that, in places, exceed the Grand Canyon in depth. By the time the Ice Age set in, the Sierra Nevada was already a fascinating landscape. Glaciers, it turns out, were simply the icing on an already remarkable cake.

ANCIENT ROCKS

YOSEMITE'S STORY BEGAN roughly 500 million years ago, when North America lay near the equator and California lay under a warm tropical sea. As rivers flowed into the sea from North America, they flushed massive amounts of sediments offshore. Over time, as the layers of sediment grew thousands of feet thick, the bottom-most layers were compressed into sedimentary rocks. Then, as tectonic plates shifted and North America rotated and moved north—a process that took hundreds of millions of years—the sedimentary rocks were pushed up to form the ancient surface of California.

Around 210 million years ago North America collided with a vast tectonic plate called the Farallon Plate, which lay under the ocean to the west. As the North American Plate overrode the Farallon Plate—a process geologists call subduction—the Farallon Plate was pushed several miles beneath North America, where extreme heat and pressure melted its leading edge. Vast pools of magma rose up under California, some of which reached the surface to form volcanoes. But most of the magma simply cooled into granite several miles below ground.

For the next 130 million years, as subduction of the Farallon Plate continued, enormous quantities of magma rose up under California in giant plumes called plutons. The plutons arrived in a series of pulses that lasted between 10 and 15 million years. By about 80 million years ago, the combined plutons formed a giant, underground mass of granite called a batholith (from the Greek words *bathos*, "deep," and *lithos*, "rock"). Throughout the formation of the Sierra Nevada Batholith, intense temperatures and pressures cooked the overlying sedimentary rocks, altering their chemical composition. Over time the sedimentary rocks were transformed (metamorphosed) into metamorphic rocks.

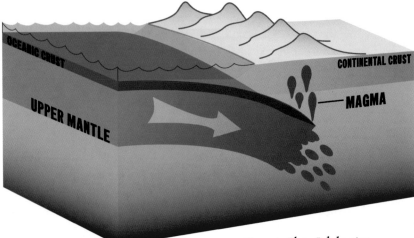

Oceanic Plate Subduction

THE MOUNTAINS RISE

AS SUBDUCTION SENT massive pools of magma rising under California, a chain of active volcanoes formed on the surface that, at their peak, may have towered as high as 18,000 feet above the landscape. But around 80 million years ago the magma stopped rising and the volcanoes became inactive. For the next 40 million years erosion slowly ground down the mountains, removing the overlying metamorphic rock and exposing the underlying granite.

As the mountains rose up, the gradients of rivers increased, speeding their flow and accelerating their erosive power. The rivers carved deep canyons and flushed millions of tons of sediment into California's Central Valley, which lies just west of the Sierra Nevada. Drive across the Central Valley today and you are driving across eroded Sierra Nevada sediments reaching depths of tens of thousands of feet.

Around 20 million years ago, the western edge of North America came into contact with an entirely new tectonic plate: the Pacific Plate, which underlies much of the Pacific Ocean. But the collision between the Pacific Plate and the North American Plate was not head-on. Rather, the plates moved laterally in opposite directions, grinding against each other along their boundary and forming the San Andreas Fault.

As the two tectonic plates scraped against each other along the San Andreas Fault, huge pressures built up among interlocking rocks. Ultimately the rocks buckled, relieving pressure and jolting the land and causing earthquakes. But not all of the built-up pressure was concentrated on the San Andreas Fault. The force of the grinding plates fanned out across California, cracking the land and forming new, smaller faults.

As a complex set of pressures exerted themselves from multiple directions, a fault system formed near the eastern edge of the Sierra Nevada Batholith. The land rose up as if on a pivot from the west, creating a sheer eastern slope and a long, gentle western slope. Uplift started slowly around 10 million years ago, then accelerated several million years later. Before long the modern Sierra Nevada towered 14,000 feet above the landscape.

Throughout the uplift of the Sierra Nevada, millions of cracks formed in the mountain's granite. Initial cracks formed due to pressures associated with uplift, followed by cracks that formed as erosion stripped away miles of overlying rocks, causing the underlying rocks to expand and crack. These cracks (called *joints*) are still forming today. Extending in every direction, they create a giant template for future erosion. Some cracks are vertical, some are horizontal, and some form in rounded concentric layers. The concentric cracks are the most fascinating, for they erode in curved sheets, flaking off like layers of an onion and leaving behind rounded domes (a process called *exfoliation*).

ICE AGE GLACIERS

AROUND 2.4 MILLION years ago, Earth entered the Ice Age. As global temperatures cooled and snowfall increased, a thick snowpack accumulated in the Sierra Nevada that, over time, compacted into massive sheets of ice. When the ice sheets were set into motion under the pressure of their own weight, they became glaciers. Pushing downhill, the glaciers consumed everything in their path. Boulders, soil, trees—everything but the bedrock was picked up and carried along. But even the bedrock did not escape unscathed. The glaciers—essentially dirty ice full of debris—acted like giant sheets of sandpaper, grinding down the bedrock and smoothing it out.

Then, abruptly, temperatures warmed and the glaciers retreated. Then they advanced and retreated again. And again. And again. Over the past 2.4 million years, as global temperatures have fluctuated, glaciers have advanced and retreated at least three times in the Sierra Nevada. At higher latitudes glaciers have advanced and retreated over a dozen times, and many geologists believe that Sierra Nevada glaciers followed a similar pattern. But because the Sierra Nevada glaciers erased everything in their path, including the evidence of previous glaciers, supporting facts are scarce.

The oldest and largest glacial advance in the Sierra Nevada, known as the pre-Tahoe glaciation, occurred roughly one million years ago. As pre-Tahoe glaciers descended from high elevations, they blanketed the mountains under a massive sheet of ice roughly 270 miles long by 40 miles wide. Only the highest peaks in the Sierra remained exposed, poking out like rocky islands in a sea of ice. All told, over half of Yosemite was covered by ice. Tuolumne Meadows was buried under 2,000 feet of ice, and Yosemite Valley was filled to the brim.

The force of the glaciers was massive. Under the largest glaciers, pressures topped several hundred pounds per square inch. Where the bedrock was weakened by cracks, glaciers plucked out large chunks of rock and carried them down to lower elevations. Where the bedrock was solid and relatively free of cracks, glaciers smoothed out the rock and formed glacial polish—a glassy veneer with a texture as smooth as polished marble. In places the glacial polish was scraped by rocks embedded at the bottom of the glacier, leaving behind distinct scratches called glacial striations.

Descending from high elevations—at speeds ranging from several inches to several feet per day—the glaciers flowed through previously formed river valleys that, cut by pre-Ice Age rivers, had steep V-shaped profiles. As the glaciers advanced through the V-shaped valleys, they gouged out the sides, leaving rounded U-shaped valleys in their wake.

As glaciers flowed down the mountains, picking up bits and pieces of the landscape along the way, the front of the ice bulldozed accumulated debris.

Glacial Erratics

When the ice reached lower, warmer elevations, the front of the glacier melted and deposited the debris. Ice continued to flow from above, however, forming a kind of conveyor belt that transported even more loose material to the melting front of the glacier. These debris piles are called terminal moraines, and they mark the farthest extent of the glacier. A similar feature, called lateral moraines, formed along the sides of the glacier. Today many remnant terminal and lateral moraines mark the maximum extent of the glaciers that deposited them.

During each of the Sierra Nevada glaciations, glaciers advanced for tens of thousands of years. But as global temperatures warmed, the glaciers melted in a fraction of that time, and large boulders embedded in the ice settled on the underlying bedrock. These rocks, often carried miles from their point of origin, are called glacial erratics. Today they are found throughout the High Sierra.

At the end of the most recent glaciation—the Tioga glaciation, which ended roughly 10,000 years ago—temperatures warmed and the glaciers started to melt. By about 8,000 years ago glaciers had completely disappeared from the Sierra Nevada. Since then, however, fluctuations in climate have triggered at least two additional periods of glacial advance and retreat (albeit on a much smaller scale). The most recent glaciation occurred from 1600 to 1850, when temperatures dropped during a period of global cooling called the Little Ice Age. During this time roughly 100 small glaciers formed in the Sierra Nevada. But over the past 150 years, as global temperatures have risen, many of those glaciers have melted. Today only a handful of small glaciers remain in the Yosemite region.

Yosemite's glacially sculpted High Sierra

At the height of the Ice Age one million years ago, only Yosemite's tallest peaks remained above the glaciers, poking out like rocky islands in a sea of ice. Although the glaciers rounded and smoothed the lower slopes of these mountains, their summits remained jagged and rough. Today these angular peaks, called nunataks, can be seen throughout the High Sierra.

GEOLOGY TODAY

GLACIERS PUT THE finishing touches on the Sierra Nevada, but erosion continues to chip away at the range. One of the most common acts of erosion is frost wedging, which occurs when water freezes and expands in the cracks of rocks, wedging and breaking them apart. Frost wedging is most active in the spring and fall when daily temperature fluctuations are greatest.

Earthquakes are also common in the Sierra Nevada, which is riddled with active faults along its eastern boundary. In 1872 an earthquake shook the ground near Lone Pine, California, which lies at the base of the eastern Sierra. The earthquake, which was probably bigger than the San Francisco earthquake of 1906, killed 27 people and pulverized nearly every building in town. In an instant the mountains above Lone Pine jumped 13 feet higher and shifted 20 feet laterally. In Yosemite Valley, the early morning earthquake woke up John Muir, who stumbled outside to watch a lofty rock pinnacle crash to the ground. An observer near Nevada Falls claimed the waterfall stopped flowing for at least half a minute, and several thousand tons of rock shook free from nearby Liberty Cap, creating a powerful air blast that knocked a nearby building off of its foundation.

Earthquakes and other forms of erosion can also trigger rockslides, which volume-wise are probably the most substantial form of erosion acting on Yosemite right now. Sometime around 1740 a massive rockslide took out 5.6 *million tons* of Slide Mountain (later named for the rock slide) in a remote, northern section of the park. Dozens of smaller rockslides have taken place since, including a 2006 whopper along the Merced River Canyon west of Yosemite Valley. That rockslide buried 600 feet of Highway 140 and closed the road for nearly two months. As the years progress, erosion will chip away at these rockslides, reducing boulders to talus, talus to scree, scree to gravel, and gravel to sand.

Parts of the eastern Sierra Nevada are also volcanically active. Mammoth Mountain, home to the popular ski resort southeast of Yosemite, is a volcano that formed 400,000 years ago. And a large magma chamber exists under Mono Basin directly east of Yosemite. The last known volcanic event in the region was a mild underwater eruption at the bottom of Mono Lake in 1890. When, or where, the next eruption will occur is unknown.

Moving forward, the forces of geology will continue to reshape the landscape. Over hundreds of years, rockfalls will continue to erode Yosemite's cliffs. Over tens of thousands of years, vast glaciers could cover the mountains again if past cycles repeat themselves. And over millions of years the park's most stunning features—Half Dome, El Capitan, Yosemite Falls—will disappear entirely. So consider yourself lucky. You're alive for that brief moment (geologically speaking) when Yosemite is filled with world-class scenery that generations of visitors have come to know and love.

Whitney Vs. Muir
The Formation of Yosemite Valley

JOHN MUIR

When members of the California State Geologic Survey first studied Yosemite Valley in the 1860s, they found themselves perplexed. Unlike most glacially carved valleys, which have a graceful U-shape, Yosemite Valley has steep, vertical cliffs rising from an essentially flat floor. Given this unusual topography, the Survey determined that the Valley was not sculpted by glaciers, but created by a sudden, cataclysmic event—perhaps an earthquake that caused the floor of Yosemite Valley to drop down.

John Muir vehemently disagreed with the Survey's "drop down" theory. Having studied the effects of glaciers during his wanderings in the High Sierra, Muir was convinced that Yosemite Valley was sculpted by glaciers. Although Muir had studied geology during his last two years at the University of Wisconsin, he was a scientific amateur, and members of the Geologic Survey brushed off his theory with amusement. Josiah Whitney, the Yale-educated head of the Survey, insisted there was no evidence that glaciers had ever occupied Yosemite Valley.

Muir was confident in his beliefs, however, and the more he "preached" (his words) the more people listened. By 1870 Muir's theories were endorsed by the famous geologist Louis Agassiz and his student Dr. Joseph Le Conte, a professor at the University of California. Members of the State Geologic Survey could not believe it. Soon they were hurling insults at Muir, calling him an "ignoramus" and "a mere sheepherder." Whitney stated that the glacier theory was "based on entire ignorance of the whole subject, [and] may be dropped without wasting any more time upon it."

In fact, the debate raged on for nearly 60 years. Then, in 1930—long after the deaths of both Whitney and Muir—the distinguished French geologist François Matthes announced that he too agreed with Muir's theory, finally laying the matter to rest. Although Muir's theory was not entirely correct, it was close. And although Whitney was wrong about Yosemite Valley, he did correctly identify Hetch Hetchy as a glacially sculpted valley. Regardless, the heated debate between Whitney and Muir soon became one of the classic amateur-beats-the-pro tales of geology.

JOSIAH WHITNEY

Running half the length of California, the Sierra Nevada is the longest, highest, and grandest mountain range in America. Although the Rockies and Appalachians are longer, they are technically mountain systems made up of several smaller ranges. The Sierra Nevada, by contrast, is a single unbroken range that is nearly as large as the French, Swiss, and Italian Alps combined. At roughly 26,000 square miles, it covers 17% of California.

From Fredonyer Pass in the north to Tehachapi Pass in the south, the Sierra Nevada stretches 420 miles, varying in width from 50 to 80 miles. The mountains are essentially a massive block of granite lifted like a trapdoor on a western hinge. The long western slope rises gradually at a tilt of just 2 to 6 degrees, while the steep eastern slope plummets 25 degrees—dropping over two miles in places. Sierra peaks increase in elevation from north to south, reaching 10,000 feet near Lake Tahoe, 13,000 feet in Yosemite, and 14,000 feet near Mt. Whitney. At 14,495 feet, Mt. Whitney is the tallest peak in the continental United States. All told, the entire range contains roughly 500 peaks above 12,000 feet. Over half of the alpine Sierra (the area located above treeline) is exposed rock, and nearly all of it is protected as national parks or federally designated wilderness.

The Sierra is bounded in the west by California's Central Valley, where flat agricultural lands grow a quarter of America's food. As coastal air flows over the Sierra from the west, moisture is wrung out of the air as it rises and cools. Stripped of its moisture, the dry air heads east over Nevada and Utah, casting a massive rain shadow over the Great Basin Desert.

Sierra summers are generally dry, but winters can dump up to 70 feet of snow. The heaviest snowfall occurs in the Central Sierra, which bears the brunt of winter storms that creep through San Francisco's Golden Gate—the most prominent gap in California's coastal mountains. In the spring a combination of rain and snowmelt brings heavy runoff to the Sierra Nevada, but by autumn many streams have slowed to a trickle.

Only a handful of rivers tumble down the Sierra's steep eastern flank. Flowing into the Great Basin Desert, their waters never reach the sea. On the gentle western slope, 11 major rivers flow into the Central Valley, eight of which join the Sacramento and San Joaquin rivers on their journey to San Francisco Bay. Many western Sierra rivers have cut dramatic valleys thousands of feet deep. The largest, Kings Canyon, is deeper than Grand Canyon with walls over 7,000 feet high.

Resting on the northern slope of Mt. Lyell—the highest peak in the park—the Lyell Glacier is the largest glacier in Yosemite. It's also the second largest glacier in the Sierra Nevada and one of the southernmost glaciers in North America. Both the mountain and the glacier are named for Charles Lyell, whose 1830 book *Principles of Geology* has been called "the most seminal work in geology." Ironically, when the theory of Ice Ages was first advanced in the 1830s, Lyell did not believe it, and he argued against it for decades.

ECOLOGY

COVERING 1,200 SQUARE miles and over 10,000 feet of mountainous elevation, Yosemite is home to thousands of fascinating plants and animals. Giant sequoias, the largest organisms on the planet, have been living at the park's mid elevations for thousands of years, while delicate alpine flowers measure their lives in weeks among the parks highest peaks. The forests in between are home to black bears, mountain lions, bobcats, deer, and dozens of smaller animals. All told, over 80 species of mammals, over 150 species of birds, and over 1,400 species of plants have been identified in the park.

Plants and animals live only where factors such as temperature, sunlight, and access to food and water favor their survival. Because plants form the foundation of a thriving food chain, ecologists have divided the Sierra Nevada into half a dozen vegetative zones—five of which occur in Yosemite. These zones, based loosely on elevation, provide an easy way to visualize a complex system. Boundaries between zones are often fuzzy, with some species living in two or three zones and with many microclimates within each zone. But such complexity is to be expected in a place where the landscape changes so fast. Driving from the arid plains of the Great Central Valley to alpine Tioga Pass—at 9,943 feet the highest paved road in California—is the ecological equivalent of driving from Mexico to Alaska in a single day.

Taken as a whole, the Sierra Nevada boasts many impressive statistics. It's the highest unbroken mountain range in the continental U.S. and the second snowiest range on the continent (after the Cascades in the Pacific Northwest). Over 3,500 plant species are found in the Sierra Nevada—a number greater than the total number plant species found in the entire state of Florida. And the alpine Sierra, which lies above treeline, has the largest, richest flora of any alpine area in North America. This high altitude wonderland is home to nearly 200 species found nowhere else in the world. But like environments everywhere, it is constantly changing. Geological forces, fluctuating climate, and human influences that started with the arrival of Indians have all shaped the present environment—and will continue to shape it in the years to come. How the modern distribution of plants and animals came to be, and how it operates today, is one of the most fascinating aspects of Yosemite.

A CHANGING LANDSCAPE

YOSEMITE'S MODERN ECOLOGY started to take shape around 15,000 years ago when Ice Age glaciers started to melt. The glaciers had scraped away soil and vegetation, and when the ice melted it revealed a barren landscape filled with expanses of smooth, glistening granite. The scenery back then must have been extraordinary—hundreds of square miles of bare granite billowing down from the highest peaks. Bedrock depressions scooped out by the glaciers filled with meltwater, creating thousands of new lakes, but much of the landscape was essentially lifeless.

The formation of soil, a combination of disintegrated rock and decomposed organic material, was an extremely slow process. Granite is one of the most erosion-resistant rocks on the planet, and organic material in the wake of the glaciers was sparse. But over thousands of years, after lichens and other hardy colonizers had gained a foothold, a thin layer of topsoil built up, making the mountains habitable for progressively larger plants. Eventually enough topsoil built up to support sun-loving trees, which thrived in the open, sunny landscape. When a shady forest canopy developed, shade-loving trees also took root.

Ecologists call this ongoing process of new plant arrival in response to changing conditions succession. In the long term, succession occurs as fluctuating climate alters temperature and precipitation, which changes the composition of forests and meadows. In the short term, succession occurs when forests are disturbed by fire, avalanches, or insect infestations. As the composition of the forest changes, so do the species of plants and animals living there. Some species thrive in sunny open spaces, while others prefer mature forests.

Over the past 10,000 years, as environmental conditions have changed, the ecology of the Sierra Nevada has changed with them. Temperatures have warmed considerably since the melting of the glaciers, but the rate of warming has not been steady. As temperatures have fluctuated, Sierra Nevada vegetation has marched up and down the mountains accordingly, shifting to higher elevations during periods of warming and retreating to lower elevations during periods of cooling. Changing climate also affects precipitation. The past 1,200 years have seen two major droughts, each lasting 100 to 200 years, while the past 150 years have been relatively warm and wet, containing one of the wettest half centuries of the past 1,000 years. All of this, combined with modern human influences, has affected forest density and wildfire patterns, laying the groundwork for the present forest composition.

Although area-wise the Sierra Nevada covers just 20 percent of California, the mountains contain over half of California's 7,000 plant species. Roughly one-third of Sierra plant species are endemic (found nowhere else in the world).

ECOLOGY TODAY

YOSEMITE'S MODERN ECOLOGY is characterized by five broad vegetation zones based loosely on elevation: foothill woodlands, mixed conifer forests, upper montane forest, subalpine zone, and the alpine zone. These zones are also influenced by latitude, which effects temperature and precipitation. As one moves north or south from Yosemite, these zones shifts lower and higher respectively.

Summers in the Sierra Nevada are hot and dry, resulting in less than five percent of the region's annual precipitation. Winters, however, dump massive amounts of snow—up to 50 feet in some places—with over 95 percent of the Sierra's annual precipitation falling between October and April.

Seasonal weather in the Sierra Nevada is more varied and dramatic than in any other mountain range in North America, which has profound implications for plants and animals living in the Sierra. After surviving summer droughts and deep winter snows, plants and animals must contend with massive runoff in the spring. Three-quarters of the Sierra snowpack melts between April and June, and the combined outflow of streams and rivers tumbling down from the Sierra Nevada is often 10 times larger than the Colorado River, which drains seven western states. But precipitation is highly variable. Runoff in very wet years can be up to 20 *times* greater than runoff in very dry years.

Thousands of streams flow down from the Sierra Nevada, coalescing into 11 major rivers on the western slope. Yosemite is home to two of the Sierra's most impressive rivers: the Merced and the Tuolumne, which drain 511 square miles and 680 square miles respectively within the park. All told, over 1,600 miles of streams flow through Yosemite.

When white settlers arrived in Yosemite in the mid-1800s, there were no fish above 6,000 feet due to natural barriers such as waterfalls and steep gradients. But in the late 1800s trout and other non-natives were intentionally introduced to dozens of lakes in Yosemite. In the early days fish were placed in 10-gallon milk cans and hauled up the mountains by mule; later fish were dropped from planes into mountain lakes. Introduced fish made tasty meals for anglers but disrupted native ecosystems. The populations of many amphibian species declined as the new arrivals feasted on frogs and tadpoles. Although fish stocking was halted in Yosemite in the 1980s, trout continue to thrive in many high altitude lakes—and amphibian populations continue to decline. A recent drop in mountain yellow-legged frog populations has also been attributed to the deadly chytrid fungus (linked to declining amphibian populations worldwide) and to pesticides blown in from the Central Valley.

YOSEMITE VEGETATIVE ZONES

FOOTHILL WOODLANDS (500 - 3,000 feet)

The foothill woodlands, found only at Yosemite's lowest elevations, are hot and dry in the summer, while winter brings little or no snow. Common plants include manzanita, interior live oak, Douglas (blue) oak, gray pine, and many drought-resistant shrubs collectively called chaparral. (The word chaparral is derived from the Spanish *chaparro* " scrub oak.") The foothill woodlands are well adapted to natural fire, passing through frequent cycles of burning and regrowth.

LOWER MONTANE FORESTS (3,000 - 6,000 feet)

Lower montane forests cover 166,000 acres in Yosemite, including Yosemite Valley, Wawona, and Big Oak Flat Road. This zone experiences hot, dry summers and cool winters that often bring several feet of snow. Dry slopes are dominated by ponderosa pine; wet slopes harbor white fir. Other species include sugar pine, incense cedar, black oak, and giant sequoia. Frequent natural fires historically favored the development of ponderosa-dominated forests throughout the lower montane zone.

UPPER MONTANE FOREST (6,000 - 8,000 feet)

This zone, covering 216,000 acres in Yosemite, is characterized by cool summers and cold, snowy winters. Typical trees include pure stands of red fir and lodgepole pine. Other species include western juniper and Jeffrey pine (which has bark that smells like vanilla or butterscotch). The upper montane forest is also noteworthy for its gorgeous meadows filled with blooming wildflowers between June and August.

SUBALPINE SIERRA NEVADA (8,000 - 10,400 feet)

This is Yosemite's largest vegetative zone, covering 297,000 acres. It's also the official start of the High Sierra, defined as the region above 8,000 feet. The subalpine zone is characterized by short cool summers and long snowy winters. Tree species include lodgepole pine, mountain hemlock, western white pine, and white bark pine. Lightning strikes are common, but large fires are rare due to the short fire season and frequent natural fire breaks such as meadows and rock outcrops.

ALPINE SIERRA NEVADA (10,400 - 13,000 feet)

Covering 54,300 acres above treeline in Yosemite, the alpine Sierra Nevada is a harsh, rocky landscape where snow covers the ground for most of the year. Summer is measured in weeks, and only hardy plants flourish during the brief growing season. Compared to other alpine areas of comparable latitude in North America, the Sierra Nevada alpine zone is drier than most in the summer, wetter than most in the winter, and warmer than most throughout the year.

COMMON YOSEMITE TREES

PONDEROSA PINE
(Pinus ponderosa)

Ponderosa pines are the most common western conifer, with a distribution that roughly outlines the American West. In the central Sierra they grow at elevations between 3,000 and 6,000 feet, and mature trees can attain heights of 225 feet. Needles grow in bunches of three. The ponderosa's defining characteristic is its pale yellowish bark, which forms large interlocking plates that can look like pieces of a jigsaw puzzle.

INCENSE CEDAR
(Calocedrus decurrens)

Incense cedars, distinguished by their thick stringy bark, grow up to 150 feet tall. Needles are small, flat, and waxy. The tree's fragrant wood is famous for its use in pencils. A highly versatile conifer, it is able to germinate and grow in both sunny and shady areas. Although once scarce in Yosemite Valley, several decades of fire suppression have allowed incense cedars to flourish.

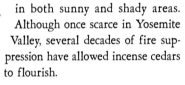

LODGEPOLE PINE
(Pinus contorta)

Lodgepole pines (named by Lewis & Clark, who observed Indians using them to build lodges) can grow up to 125 feet high. Needles grow in bunches of two. Lodgepoles generally grow between 6,000 and 10,000 feet in the central Sierra Nevada, but occasionally they are found at lower elevations, including Yosemite Valley. The tree's cornflake-like bark flakes off in scales and is among the thinnest of any pine.

At the park's highest elevations, lakes and ponds support fewer plants and animals due to a lack of nutrients. Alpine lakes and ponds are considered biologically poor because surrounding vegetation is sparse and organic debris is limited. Many alpine lakes have a striking turquoise color, however, due to glacial flour—extremely fine rock particles ground down by glaciers. Glacial flour is flushed into high elevation lakes where, suspended in the otherwise clear water, it reflects blue and green wavelengths of light.

At lower elevations with more vegetation, lakes are richer with organic debris, and thus support a thriving food chain. But over time, as organic debris accumulates and sediments are deposited by tributary streams, the lakes slowly fill in. Many low elevation meadows are former lakes that filled with sediment and organic debris, and many of these meadows will ultimately be invaded by saplings and trees.

Although soil fertility in the Sierra Nevada is generally poor due to the short, dry growing season, it is one of the most productive sites for conifers in the world. Nearly half of all trees in the Sierra Nevada are conifers. (By comparison, conifers represent just 10% of trees in the Southeastern U.S.) Most of the bedrock in the Sierra Nevada is granite, which breaks down into soil that is coarse-grained and granular. The soil, which lacks much clay, drains very easily, and throughout much of the Sierra Nevada soils are thin, rocky and dry—perfect for conifers.

Lodgepole pine forests dominate much of Yosemite's high country, covering over 150,000 acres in the park. Although large fires are rare in lodgepole forests, lodgepoles periodically succumb to insect infestations caused by the lodgepole needle miner, a tiny moth that lays its eggs in lodgepole pine needles. Larvae feed on the needles—killing them in the process—and moths emerge in July of odd-numbered years. This two-year life cycle deters predators and allows thousands of moths to swarm over the landscape. Large-scale infestations kill thousands of trees, creating extensive stands of still-standing dead trees. These "ghost forests" cover roughly 40,000 acres in Yosemite due to an outbreak that started in 1973. In recent years the outbreak has swept around the southern flank of the Cathedral Range, arriving at Sunrise High Sierra Camp in 2001.

Roughly 90 percent of the Sierra Nevada is covered in vegetation. Forests dominate Yosemite's scenery from the park's lowest elevations up to treeline, which occurs at roughly 10,400 feet. Treeline is determined by a number of factors—soil, precipitation, wind, length of growing season—but its limiting factor is cold. If a certain area is too cold, no tree will survive, no matter how favorable the other conditions. Surprisingly, it's not winter cold but summer cold that determines treeline. Although Sierra trees can survive temperatures much colder than those experienced in an average winter, they cannot withstand those temperatures year-round. Summer temperatures must average 50° Fahrenheit or greater for a tree to grow. If a certain location experiences average July temperatures below 50 degrees, no trees will grow there.

YOSEMITE WILDFLOWERS

Harlequin Lupine
Lupinus stiversii

Mountain Pride Penstemon
Penstemon newberryi

Small Leopard Lily
Lilium parvum

Wild Iris
Iris missouriensis

Coville's Columbine
Aquilegia pubescens

Mariposa Lily
Calochortus leichtlinii

Treeline is a loose boundary, however, with short scraggly trees finding a way to scrape out a living above 10,400 feet. Some trees grow at dwarf sizes. Others put down roots in warm microclimates that allow them to grow at slightly higher elevations. The absolute limit of treeline, above which no tree can possibly grow, is called the krummholz limit (*krummholz* is the German word for "twisted tree"). In Yosemite, whitebark pine dominates treeline, along with shrubs such as willows, buckwheats, and currants.

Above treeline is the alpine zone—a harsh, beautiful landscape filled with the Sierra's famous sparkling granite. The Sierra Nevada alpine zone stretches over 150 unbroken miles from Mt. Whitney to Sonora Pass, just north of Yosemite. Many hikers and backpackers consider this region to be the most spectacular part of Yosemite, but heavy snow covers the landscape for most of the year, making it accessible only in the summer and fall. Due to the short growing season, plants in the alpine zone flower and fruit much faster than their low-elevations counterparts, and their reproductive cycle is condensed into weeks instead of months. Plants are very active during the summer, photosynthesizing rapidly during the long, sunny days before cold temperatures once again descend.

Animals in the alpine zone have also adapted to the inhospitable landscape. Many alpine mammals have thick fur and rounded bodies that maximize volume and minimize of heat loss. But when winter arrives, most animals in the alpine zone descend to lower, warmer elevations in search of food. Only a few hardy animals remain in the alpine zone year-round.

THE IMPORTANCE OF FIRE

WHEN EUROPEANS FIRST arrived in the Sierra Nevada, they marveled at the sunny, open forests they encountered. Trees were spaced widely apart, and the forest floor was relatively free of debris. According to one early report, you could ride a horse through the forest at full gallop. While this was not true of the entire Sierra, open forests were an important of the mix. Unknown to the Europeans, these beautiful, park-like landscapes were the result of frequent fires.

Small, natural fires caused by lightning strikes historically swept through low and mid-elevation Sierra Nevada forests about once every decade or so, and they played an important role in the ecosystem. Regular fires clear out brush and forest debris, return nutrients to the soil, reduce insect pests, and destroy young saplings that would otherwise compete with older trees. Large trees, protected by thick bark, not only survive small fires, many thrive in the fire's wake. In the course of a typical year, it was not uncommon for thousands of acres to burn in the Sierra Nevada, although fires at high elevations were much less common.

Indians, expert observers of the natural world, understood the benefits of fire. For thousands of years they set intentional fires to maintain open forests and meadows. This reduced the buildup of underbrush and saplings, which could otherwise fuel catastrophic wildfires that had the potential to destroy large tracts of forest. In some areas this was of critical importance. The loss of acorn-producing oak trees, for example, could devastate a tribe's food supply. Regular, small fires also created optimum habitat for the animals that Indians liked to hunt and produced wide open spaces that made hunting much easier. According to one Sierra Miwok elder, "the Indians used to burn in the fall—October and November. They set the fires from the bottom of the slope to decrease the snowpack, get rid of the debris so there's no fire danger and they burned in the hunting areas so there was more food for the deer. They burned every year and in the same areas." To the Indians, fire was a potent landscaping tool.

When Indian populations were decimated by disease and genocide, Indian-set fires became increasingly rare in the Sierra. In the 1870s Stephen Powers noted that historic forests "were more open and park-like than at present." Then, in the mid-1800s, sheepherders began setting frequent fires in the mountains to keep meadows open and increase the number of edible grasses for grazing animals. According to one sheepherder, "We started setting fires and continued setting them until we reached the foothills. We burned everything that would burn." The resulting smoke and haze infuriated many local residents including John Muir, who noted, "The entire forest belt is thus swept and devastated from one extremity of the range to the other." (In fairness, Muir recognized the benefits of natural fire, but he opposed human-caused fires.) Muir's feelings were echoed by Fresno resident C. M. Dabney, who complained that sheepherders, "pay no taxes, have no homes, defy our laws, and who say they do not understand English," adding that they "burn these magnificent forests as they go along." Such attitudes helped lay the groundwork for the first state laws prohibiting the setting of fires—laws that ultimately carried over to the federal level.

By the late 1890s, when Yosemite and Sequoia National Parks were established, the U.S. Army (which then administered the parks) established a policy of fire suppression to preserve and protect the landscape. The way they saw it, fire marred the scenery, threatened wildlife, and contaminated watersheds. When the U.S. Forest Service was established in 1905, it followed the Army's lead, putting out fires throughout much of the Sierra Nevada. The National Park Service, established in 1916, adopted this policy as well. Although the wisdom of fire suppression was questioned by some, it became the dominant forest policy for the next half century.

Government sponsored fire suppression, combined with a lack of Indian-set fires, soon produced the lowest fire frequencies of the past several thousand years in the Sierra Nevada. In places, natural burning of some species was reduced by 98 percent. As a result, many previously open forests became choked with thick brush and young saplings normally removed by fire. Eventually a shady canopy developed that allowed shade-loving trees such as white fir and incense cedar to invade the landscape. Saplings also invaded many mountain meadows, which had historically been kept open by fire. By 1944—the year Smokey Bear was introduced by the Forest Service to teach children the dangers of forest fire (without making any distinction between natural and man-made fires)—much of the Sierra Nevada was overgrown and, in many ways, unnatural.

A handful of researchers who studied forest fires in the 1930s concluded that fire was beneficial and necessary, but their work did not influence official forest policy. Then, in the 1950s and 60s, researchers studying the effect of fire suppression realized the severity of the situation. According to one government report, "Today, much of the west slope [of the Sierra] is a dog-hair thicket of young pines, white fir, and incense cedar, and mature brush—a direct function of overprotection from natural fires." Overgrown forests reduced habitat for many woodland animals, and the massive amount of water consumed by new vegetation reduced stream flows and lowered water tables. Perhaps most alarming, all that new growth had the potential to fuel large, severe fires that could kill mature trees, leveling large swaths of forest. Many low and mid-elevation Sierra Nevada forests were, quite literally, sitting on a tinderbox. This time, the policy makers took note.

Starting in the late 1960s, government officials authorized a regiment of closely monitored prescribed burns in southern Sierra forests. The burns duplicated the small natural fires of the past, reduced fuel loads and fire hazards, diversified habitat, returned nutrients to the soil, and allowed fire-adapted plants to regrow. The burns were a success, and in 1968 prescribed burns were initiated in Yosemite and Sequoia. In 1974 the Forest Service followed suit.

Today prescribed burns are an important part of returning many Sierra Nevada forests to a pre-fire suppression state. Burns are closely monitored by trained professionals, and they are conducted only when conditions are safe (generally in the spring or fall). The park service also allows natural, lightning-caused fires to burn, although they are closely monitored to ensure that they don't grow out of control. Visitors are often disappointed to encounter smokey, summer fires obscuring Yosemite's gorgeous views. But smoke is a natural part of the landscape. It's estimated that, historically, roughly 16,000 of Yosemite's 749,000 acres burned each year.

In addition to carefully monitored wildfires and prescribed burns, fire managers also use chainsaws to thin out dense thickets near developed areas. All three tools—fire suppression, natural burns, and mechanical thinning—are needed to return forests to their natural state, a process that will ultimately take decades. Fortunately, it is an achievable goal. When the damage of fire suppression has finally been minimized, natural fires will once again maintain the landscape in Yosemite, much as they have for thousands of years.

GIANT SEQUOIA
(Sequoiadendron giganteum)

In a park filled with superlatives, the giant sequoia remains an unforgettable sight. Capable of weighing over *two million* pounds, it's the largest organism on the planet—ever. Reaching a maximum height of 320 feet, sequoias are not the tallest tree in the world (coastal redwoods can grow up to 370 feet) but in terms of mass the giant sequoia reigns supreme. The base of a mature sequoia can reach over *35 feet* in diameter.

Giant sequoias can live up to 3,200 years. Virtually imperishable, mature trees are immune to almost all known pests and diseases. The most common cause of death is toppling over. Although the tree's thick, spongy bark is extremely fire-resistant, the green crown is flammable. Still, up to 90% of the crown can be damaged by fire and the tree will continue to grow. When fire damage disrupts the trunk's water supply, the top of the tree dies back in response, leaving behind a "snag top" common on many older trees. Fire is ultimately beneficial to the tree, however, for the heat of a fire causes cones to dry out and release their seeds. (Seeds can also be released by nibbling animals.) On average, small natural fires sweep through giant sequoia groves every 15 years.

Mature giant sequoias have up to 11,000 cones, and each cone contains about 200 tiny seeds weighing less than 1/5,000 of an ounce. But the odds of a seed growing into an adult tree are outrageously slim. Seedlings require an ideal set of circumstances: recently burned soil, sunny open space (often provided by fire), and access to abundant water. Even if every one of those conditions is met, over 99% of seedlings will die within their first two years. Those that do survive grow tall and pointy for the first 100 years, then develop a rounded crown over the next few centuries. Giant sequoias reach a maximum height around 800 years—past that age they only grow outward as they continue to add bulk.

Giant sequoias first appeared roughly 175 million years ago during the age of dinosaurs. They are members of the redwood family, which are found only in the U.S. and Asia. Giant sequoias are found exclusively on the western slope of the Sierra Nevada, occupying a range only 260 miles long by 15 miles wide. There are 75 known groves, and they generally occur between 5,000 and 7,000 feet. There are three giant sequoia groves in Yosemite (p.218, 291). Local Indians supposedly called the giant trees *wah-wo-nah*, an imitation of a hooting owl, considered the guardian spirit of the trees. The name "sequoia" is derived, strangely enough, from the Cherokee Indian Sequoyah, who developed a written version of his people's language.

Giant
Sequoia

Blue
Whale

Man

BELDING'S GROUND SQUIRREL

Spermophilus beldingi

The adorable Belding's ground squirrel lives in alpine meadows above 5,000 feet. When not nibbling on grasses or flowers, it often sits erect on its haunches, earning it the nickname "picket pin" squirrel. Belding's ground squirrels have one of the longest hibernation periods of any North American mammal (7–8 months). They are active almost exclusively during the summer months. To prepare for their long hibernation, they eat nonstop from the spring through the fall, doubling their weight and increasing their body fat by a factor of 15. Males emerge from hibernation about two weeks before females, tunneling through snow to reach the surface. Females emerge when the snow has melted, and within six days they are ready to mate—but only for three to six hours during a single day. Competition for females among males is so fierce that injuries are common and sometimes fatal. Females mate with several males, then give birth to a litter about a month later. By late August male pups have moved away from their birthplace. Females, meanwhile, remain where they were born, with several generations sharing an ancestral site.

U.S. RANGE

Found in Yosemite meadows above 5,000 feet

INFO

LENGTH: 10 to 12 inches

WEIGHT: 7 to 10 ounces

LIFESPAN: 3 to 6 years

LITTER SIZE: 5 to 8 pups

BIGHORN SHEEP

Ovis canadensis

Bighorn sheep are some of the most impressive animals in the park. Well-adapted to alpine terrain, they can hop along narrow ledges and jump down 20-foot inclines with grace. The ram's legendary horns take up to a decade to grow, curving up and over the ears in a C-shaped curl. A large pair of horns can weigh up to 30 pounds and reach 30 inches in length. During mating season, competing rams charge each other head on at speeds topping 20 mph. When the rams collide, their horns smash together and produce a loud cracking sound that can be heard for miles. Thickened skulls allow rams to withstand repeated collisions, and rams with the biggest horns generally do the most mating. Prior to European settlement, dozens of bighorn sheep herds roamed the Sierra Nevada. By 1950, however, only five herds remained due to hunting and diseases transmitted from domestic sheep. In the 1980s a bighorn recovery program established several new herds, including one near the eastern boundary of Yosemite National Park. Today there are roughly 250 bighorns in the Sierra Nevada.

U.S. RANGE

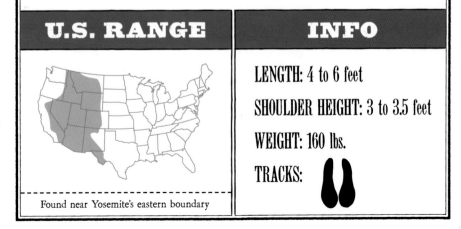

Found near Yosemite's eastern boundary

INFO

LENGTH: 4 to 6 feet

SHOULDER HEIGHT: 3 to 3.5 feet

WEIGHT: 160 lbs.

TRACKS:

BLACK BEAR

Ursus americanus

There are roughly 22,000 black bears in California, and 300 to 500 black bears in Yosemite. Despite their name, black bears in Yosemite are often dark brown or cinnamon in color. The name is derived from black bears in the eastern U.S. and Pacific Northwest where the species sports a rich black coat. Black bears have a voracious appetite, often doubling their weight by winter to prepare for hibernation. They eat grasses in the spring, berries in the summer, acorns in the fall, and ants, termites, and insect larvae whenever they can. Intelligent and adaptable, some Yosemite black bears have changed their behavior to seek out a new delicacy: food scavenged from coolers and backpacks. Such "corrupted" bears have led to strict rules regarding food storage in the park (p.34). Although generally docile, hungry bears and mothers with cubs can be dangerous. Females breed about every two years. Mating occurs in the summer, but embryos do not gestate until the mother puts on adequate weight to survive the winter. Cubs are born while the mother "lightly" hibernates, and youngsters stay with their mother until about 1.5 years in age.

U.S. RANGE

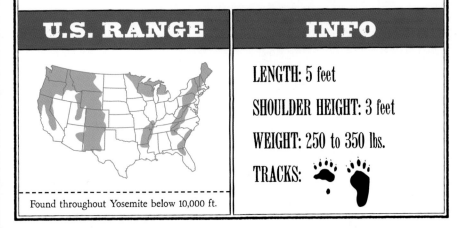

Found throughout Yosemite below 10,000 ft.

INFO

LENGTH: 5 feet

SHOULDER HEIGHT: 3 feet

WEIGHT: 250 to 350 lbs.

TRACKS:

COYOTE

Canis latrans

Nocturnal by nature, coyotes are seldom seen in Yosemite during the day, but their haunting howl often echoes through the park at night. Historically confined to the open spaces of the West, coyotes spread rapidly throughout the country following the extermination of wolves in the 1800s. Intelligent animals with a knack for scavenging, coyote populations have increased despite years of being hunted, poisoned, and trapped. Much of this success is due to an amazing reproductive response: whenever coyote populations decline, the remaining animals produce larger litters. Coyotes are also legendary opportunists that will eat just about anything: mice, squirrels, rabbits, frogs, snakes, lizards, plants, insects, garbage, etc. Unlike wolves, coyotes do not gather in large packs. Instead they usually hunt alone or in pairs. The basic social unit is two parents plus offspring less than a year old. The name "coyote" is derived from the Nahuatl (Aztec) word *cóyotl*, which may have meant "singing dog." Coyote's Latin name, *Canis latrans*, means "barking dog."

U.S. RANGE

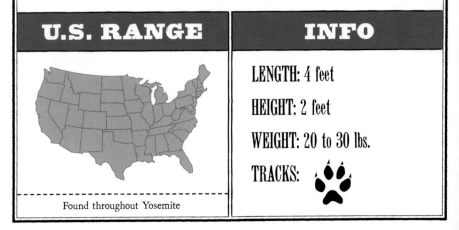

Found throughout Yosemite

INFO

LENGTH: 4 feet

HEIGHT: 2 feet

WEIGHT: 20 to 30 lbs.

TRACKS:

MOUNTAIN LION

Felis concolor

Mountain lions are the largest wildcats in North America. Among Sierra Nevada carnivores, they are second in size only to black bears. Mountain lions are rarely seen in Yosemite, but use extreme caution if you do encounter one. Also known as pumas or cougars, mountain lions have the most extensive range of any North American mammal—stretching from Canada to Argentina. At one time they inhabited all 48 lower states, but in the late 1800s and early 1900s mountain lions in the United States were hunted to the brink of extinction. Following strict hunting regulations, they have made a steady comeback in some wilderness areas. They are quick, efficient killers that can travel up to 25 miles a day in search of prey, stalking animals to within 30 feet before attacking. When they pounce they can leap up to 25 feet in a single bound, killing their victims by inflicting a lethal bite that severs the spinal cord. Mule deer are their favorite and principle prey. Male mountain lions have a home range of 64 square miles, which, marked off by urine and other scents, never overlaps with the home range of another male.

U.S. RANGE

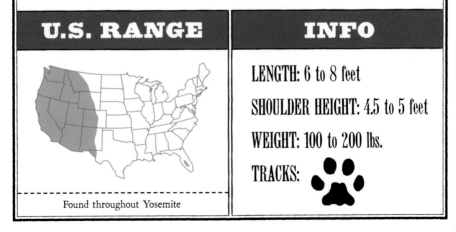

Found throughout Yosemite

INFO

LENGTH: 6 to 8 feet

SHOULDER HEIGHT: 4.5 to 5 feet

WEIGHT: 100 to 200 lbs.

TRACKS:

MULE DEER

Odocoileus hemionus

Mule deer are the most commonly spotted large mammal in the park. They are frequently seen grazing in Yosemite Valley and Tuolumne Meadows. Although closely related to white-tailed deer, mule deer are slightly larger and have white tails with a black tip. Mule deer are found throughout the Sierra Nevada. They are named for their large ears that move independently of one another, like the ears of a mule. Bucks grow antlers that are shed each winter. Although conflict between bucks in infrequent, mild fights sometimes break out. During these fights antlers are enmeshed while each buck tries to force the head of the other buck down. Injuries are rare, but if the antlers become locked both bucks will be unable to feed and will ultimately die of starvation. Fights between does are much more common, so family groups tend to be spaced widely apart. Does commonly give birth to twins in June, and fawns have white spots on their coat that last until they molt into their winter coat. Fawns are able to distinguish their mother from other does through a unique odor produced by glands on the mother's hind legs.

U.S. RANGE

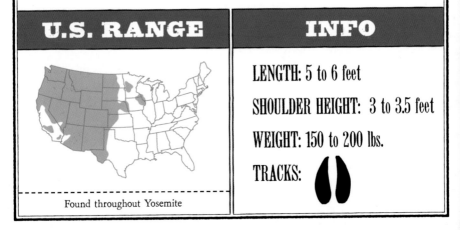

Found throughout Yosemite

INFO

LENGTH: 5 to 6 feet

SHOULDER HEIGHT: 3 to 3.5 feet

WEIGHT: 150 to 200 lbs.

TRACKS:

PEREGRINE FALCON

Falco peregrinus

Peregrine falcons are birds of prey that can spot victims from thousands of feet above. Once a target is selected, the peregrine dive bombs it at speeds topping 200 mph. The collision creates an explosion of feathers, and victims that don't die immediately upon impact have their necks broken by the peregrine's specially designed beak. Peregrines are such successful strikers that they were used to kill Nazi carrier pigeons in World War II. By the early 1970s, however, peregrine falcons sat at the brink of extinction. The extinction of the passenger pigeon (an important source of food) and the toxic effects of the pesticide DDT reduced the worldwide population to less than 40 known pairs. To save the remaining birds, young peregrines were raised in captivity and released in the wild. Today there are roughly 1,600 nesting pairs in North America. Peregrines choose nest sites (aeries) on tall cliffs, and several popular cliffs in Yosemite are off-limits to rock climbers from February through August to protect nesting falcons. In 1999 peregrines were removed from the federal Endangered Species list, but their status remains endangered in California.

U.S. RANGE

INFO

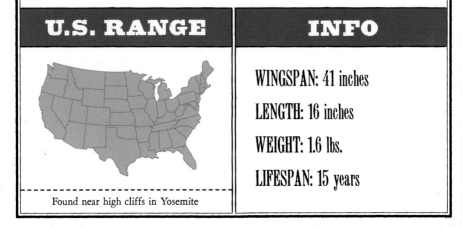

Found near high cliffs in Yosemite

WINGSPAN: 41 inches

LENGTH: 16 inches

WEIGHT: 1.6 lbs.

LIFESPAN: 15 years

STELLER'S JAY

Cyanocitta stelleri

Steller's Jays are one of the most commonly seen birds in the park, especially when food is present (as nearly any Yosemite picnicker can attest). Native to western North America, they are closely related to blue jays, but with a black crest and a blue body. Along with crows, jays, and magpies are considered one of the most intelligent birds. Stellar's Jays are omnivores that will eat just about anything, including pine nuts, fruits, seeds, insects, bird eggs, and even young birds. They can harvest up to 400 acorns per hour from the canopies of oak trees. Stellar's Jays stay in an area year-round, and they typically live in flocks of 10 or more. They must constantly stay alert for Goshawks, however, which dive bomb Steller's Jays and kill them with their feet in a vice-like grip. Steller's Jays are named after the German naturalist Georg Steller. Renowned for their loud vocalizations, their call has been described as a "very harsh, unmusical, descending *shaaaar.*" According to some reports, they can also imitate the cry of the Red-tailed Hawk, which causes other birds to abandon a feeding area as the Steller's Jay approaches.

U.S. RANGE

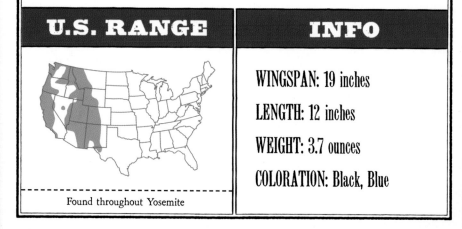

Found throughout Yosemite

INFO

WINGSPAN: 19 inches

LENGTH: 12 inches

WEIGHT: 3.7 ounces

COLORATION: Black, Blue

YELLOW-BELLIED MARMOT

Marmota flaviventris

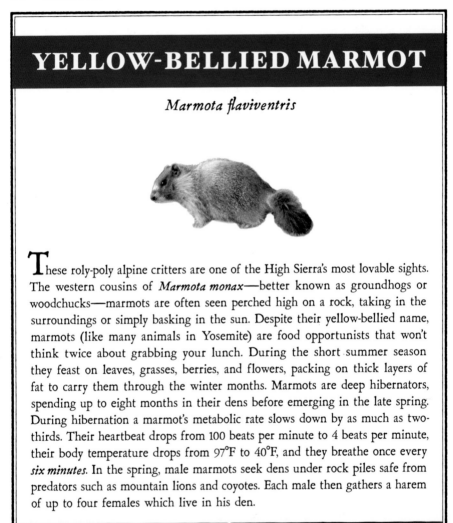

These roly-poly alpine critters are one of the High Sierra's most lovable sights. The western cousins of *Marmota monax*—better known as groundhogs or woodchucks—marmots are often seen perched high on a rock, taking in the surroundings or simply basking in the sun. Despite their yellow-bellied name, marmots (like many animals in Yosemite) are food opportunists that won't think twice about grabbing your lunch. During the short summer season they feast on leaves, grasses, berries, and flowers, packing on thick layers of fat to carry them through the winter months. Marmots are deep hibernators, spending up to eight months in their dens before emerging in the late spring. During hibernation a marmot's metabolic rate slows down by as much as two-thirds. Their heartbeat drops from 100 beats per minute to 4 beats per minute, their body temperature drops from 97°F to 40°F, and they breathe once every *six minutes*. In the spring, male marmots seek dens under rock piles safe from predators such as mountain lions and coyotes. Each male then gathers a harem of up to four females which live in his den.

U.S. RANGE

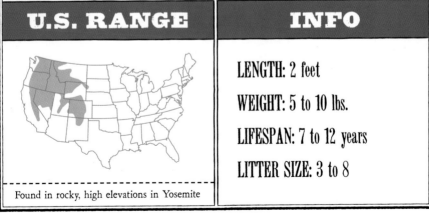

Found in rocky, high elevations in Yosemite

INFO

LENGTH: 2 feet

WEIGHT: 5 to 10 lbs.

LIFESPAN: 7 to 12 years

LITTER SIZE: 3 to 8

HISTORY

THE FIRST PEOPLE to encounter Yosemite were the Sierra Miwok Indians, who lived throughout the central Sierra Nevada for thousands of years. To the Indians, Yosemite Valley must have seemed like paradise on earth: a fortress-like hideaway filled with fresh water, edible plants, and wild game. They called the Valley Ahwahnee, "Place Like A Gaping Mouth," and the Miwok living there became known as the Ahwahneechee, "People of the Ahwahnee."

The Valley's abundant natural resources supported roughly 200 people—a fraction of the estimated 100,000 Indians living throughout the Sierra Nevada, but still relatively large for a single location. Over 35 Ahwahneechee living sites have been identified in Yosemite Valley, including permanent and temporary villages, as well as seasonal hunting and fishing camps. The largest and most important village, Koomine, was located near the base of Yosemite Falls.

During the hot summer months the Ahwahneechee wore few clothes. Men covered themselves with a single piece of deerskin folded about the hips, women wore a two-piece buckskin skirt, and children went naked until they were about 10 years old. Important villagers decorated themselves with buckskin sashes, and decorated their hair with wildflowers. When temperatures dropped, the Ahwahneechee wrapped themselves in animal-skin robes. Although the Ahwahneechee went barefoot in the village during the warmer months, they wore moccasins lined with cedar bark in the winter. Snowshoes, fashioned out of split saplings, were also used for winter travel in the High Sierra.

Edible plants, gathered by Ahwahneechee women, made up most of the tribe's diet. Greens and bulbs were harvested in the spring, seeds and fruits in the summer, and acorns in the fall. All told, over 100 plant species were harvested. In bountiful years excess crops were dried and placed in storage. In lean years Indians turned to alternate crops and traded for food with neighboring tribes, including the Mono, Yokuts, and Midou. In exchange for Ahwahneechee acorns, berries, baskets, and arrow shafts, the neighboring tribes traded salt, pinyon pine nuts, red pigment for paint, and obsidian (volcanic glass) used for arrowheads.

Although acorns and other wild crops were the tribe's main source of food, they also hunted wild animals. Hunting was the responsibility of Ahwahneechee males. When hunting alone, Indians often wore a disguise to blend in with the scenery. The most impressive disguise was the entire skin of a buck (complete with antler-shaped twigs) that the hunter wrapped around his body. The disguise, believed to hold magical powers, was put it on in secret and kept hidden between hunting ceremonies to avoid contamination by women and children. In the field, the disguised hunter mimicked the movements of a deer until he was accepted by a herd.

In their free time, both men and women played a sport similar to lacrosse with basket rackets and a buckskin ball shot through willow goal posts. Villagers also gambled on archery tournaments, footraces, and spear throwing contests. Ceremonies and rituals were common throughout the year, and in the spring and fall special "world-renewing ceremonies" were held to bring rain, maintain bountiful crops, provide animals for hunting, and prevent natural disasters.

According to early Yosemite settler Galen Clark, the Ahwahneechee were polygamists. Women were considered property, and parents sold their young daughters to the highest suitable bidder. Payment for a bride was considered an important part of the marriage ceremony. Wealthy men often had two or three wives, and once married a husband could sell or gamble his wife away—though such occurrences were said to be rare. If a woman was unfaithful to her husband, she was punished with death.

Although generally peaceful, the Ahwahneechee occasionally waged war with neighboring tribes. Galen Clark described them as "perhaps the most war-like of any of the tribes in this part of the Sierra Nevada Mountains, who were, as a rule, a peaceful people." Most disputes were settled through negotiation, but when negotiation failed the tribes resorted to violence.

Ahwahneechee Dwellings

In the summer the Ahwahneechee slept outside under an open arbor, but in the winter they lived in large, conical huts made of heavy cedar bark strips placed closely together. The entrance always faced east to greet the rising sun, and a central fire kept the structure warm. According to one observer, "there is no other form of a single-room dwelling that can be kept warm and comfortable in cold weather with so little fire."

Ahwahneechee Basketry

Basketmaking, a task performed only by women, was one of the most important aspects of Ahwahneechee culture. In the absence of pottery, baskets were essential to daily life. There were dozens of baskets with hundreds of uses: storing food, collecting trash, transporting firewood, trapping fish, etc. Baskets were given as gifts and buried with the dead, and basketry skills helped determine a woman's social status within the tribe. Ahwahneechee women were such skilled weavers that many of their baskets were watertight.

Serving more than just practical needs, basketry was a form of self-expression with important symbolic meanings. Ahwahneechee women wove beautiful baskets decorated with beads and feathers, and top basketmakers were as dexterous as professional musicians, often weaving into old age long after their eyesight had failed. Basketry was a combination of technical skill and encyclopedic botanical knowledge. Plants left to grow wild produced inferior weaving products, so Indians cultivated plants through burning and pruning to produce the longest, straightest fibers. The quality of fibers also depended on the timing of the harvest. Such intimate botanical knowledge, mastered over thousands of years, was passed down each generation from mother to daughter.

Not merely a casual way to pass the time, basketmaking was a full-blown industry in the Sierra Nevada. Roughly 50 percent of harvested plants were used to make baskets. Large, complex baskets often required thousands of shoots, and over the course of a year an entire village might require hundreds of thousands of shoots from various plants. Such demand could only satisfied through large-scale harvesting practices. Most basketry materials also required prolonged storage of one to three years to properly season the fibers, which meant weavers had to plan their basketry needs several years in advance.

EUROPEAN DISCOVERY

I N 1542 JUAN Rodríguez Cabrillo sailed north from Mexico to become the first non-Indian to explore California. Just south of present-day Monterrey he spied snow-capped mountains in the distance and described them as *las sierra nevada*, "The Snowy Range." But the mountains he saw were not the present-day Sierra Nevada, which has since led to much confusion in the history of the range. It wasn't until 1776 that Pedro Font, a Spaniard who helped colonize San Francisco Bay, saw the mountains and described them as *una grand sierra nevada*, "A Great Snowy Range." That same year he produced a map of the region, labeling the mountains "Sierra Nevada."

For the next five decades the Sierra Nevada was essentially ignored. As far as the Spanish were concerned, the range was simply a massive barrier to eastern travel. Besides, the Spaniards already had their hands full along the coast; their Catholic missions were in disarray, and Mexico was threatening to revolt.

Following the Mexican War of Independence (1810-1821), Mexico gained control of California. Around this time American beaver trappers started venturing into California from the east, searching for new hunting grounds away from the overtrapped Rockies. In 1827 legendary fur trapper Jedediah Smith, fresh from blazing an overland route from the Rockies to Southern California, led two companions up and over the western slope of the Sierra Nevada. Just 27 years old, Smith became the first white man to cross the Sierra Nevada, trudging through deep spring snow just north of Yosemite.

Seven years later the U.S. Army dispatched a 58-man expedition to cross the Sierra from the east. Led by 34-year-old Joseph Walker—a man whose "chief delight" was "to explore unknown regions"—the expedition's goal was to gather basic information about California. In mid-October 1833, after leading his men across the Great Basin Desert, Joseph Walker reached the eastern base of the Sierra Nevada. By the time he arrived, winter had already blanketed the mountains in a fresh layer of snow.

Undaunted, the men scaled the sheer eastern slope. It was a grueling journey. Deep snow made travel difficult and foraging virtually impossible for the expedition's pack animals. The men, dressed in knee-length buckskin shirts and leather leggings, battled frostbite and starvation as they descended the western slope. As food supplies dwindled, the men were reduced to eating horses that died along the way. "Our situation was growing more distressing every hour," one party member wrote, "and all we now thought of was to extricate ourselves from this inhospitable region."

Pushing on, the men followed a large stream they hoped would lead them to the base of the mountains. After a short distance the stream burst through the forest and plunged over the edge of a sheer cliff. Standing on a rocky precipice, the men became the first non-Indians to set eyes on Yosemite Valley.

Pulling out a spyglass, Walker scanned the surroundings. Yosemite Valley was free of snow and in full autumn glory. Sheer cliffs, granite domes, and dramatic waterfalls towered above open forests and meadows. A sparkling river twisted through the center of the Valley. To the shivering, half-starved men, it seemed like divine intervention—the perfect place to hunt fresh meat and for their horses to graze on tall grasses. For two days the men tried to find a route down the sheer cliffs, but ultimately they concluded that it was "utterly impossible for a man to descend."

Dejected, the men spent three days bushwhacking an alternate route down the mountains. Although Walker's party never entered Yosemite Valley, the fact that they viewed it at all is a miracle. Tucked away in the heart of the Sierra Nevada, guarded on all sides by sheer cliffs and forests, Yosemite Valley is one of the most geographically well-concealed locations in California. In the mid-1800s, you would literally have to stumble upon Yosemite Valley to find it—which is exactly what the next white people did.

In October 1849 two gold miners tracked a grizzly bear just south of Yosemite. Bushwhacking through the trees, the men stumbled upon an Indian trail that led them to the entrance of Yosemite Valley. They were spellbound by the scenery. Laid out before them were "stupendous cliffs rising perhaps 3000 feet from their base which gave us cause for wonder." Content simply to savor the view, the two men never entered Yosemite Valley. Had they ventured farther they would have encountered a world virtually unchanged since the Walker expedition. In the previous two years, however, life just outside the Valley had been turned completely upside down.

THE GOLD RUSH

O N JANUARY 24, 1848, nine days before the U.S. acquired California from Mexico, a man named James Marshall noticed something sparkling in the American River in the foothills northwest of Yosemite. "It made my heart thump," he later recounted, "for I was certain it was gold." Marshall tried to keep his discovery secret, but rumors quickly spread. When local store owner Sam Brannan heard the news, he purchased enormous quantities of mining supplies. He then headed to San Francisco and waved a bottle of gold dust over his head shouting "Gold! Gold from the American River!" Within a few weeks, 75 percent of the men living in San Francisco had left town to dig for gold.

News of California's instant riches spread like wildfire across the globe. At the start of 1848, 800 people lived in San Francisco. By the end of 1849, 100,000 people had arrived in California, and thousands more were on their way. They came from Europe, China, Australia, South America—anywhere the news spread. In 1850 California demanded statehood and got it. By the end of the decade, over 300,000 people had flooded the state and two million pounds of gold (worth over $15 billion today) had been pulled out of California mines and streams.

In 1848, when miners first arrived in the foothills, local Indians greeted them with characteristic hospitality. Natives watched the mining process with great interest, and when they realized the value of the shiny metal many Indians panned for it themselves. Indians eagerly exchanged gold dust for blankets and other supplies. For a short while, everything was fine.

Then, as tens of thousands of miners poured into the foothills, the situation quickly deteriorated. Miners competed with Indians for deer and chopped down acorn-bearing oak trees—the Indians' primary source of food. Many miners were inherently distrustful of Indians, and they often confiscated Indian territory by force. Within months Indians became second class citizens in a land they had occupied for thousands of years.

Angry and starving, some Indians were reduced to raiding mining camps and trading posts. Such incidents, reported widely among miners, further fueled white suspicion, leading to a downward spiral of white-Indian relations.

Just south of Yosemite, a ruthless, charismatic man named James Savage employed hundreds of Indians to work his lucrative mining claims. A former cattle thief, Savage turned his attention to gold when the news broke, and soon he oversaw a small empire of gold mines and trading posts. By 1850 he was earning roughly $20,000 a day. To ensure the Indians' goodwill, he learned their language, adopted their customs, and married the daughters of several chiefs. He also intimidated the Indians through claims of supernatural powers. According to one story, he once let an Indian shoot at him with a gun filled with six blanks. As each shot went off, Savage made a grabbing gesture in the air. When the smoke cleared, Savage produced six bullets in his hands—proof, he declared, that guns

could not hurt him. According to one observer, "Jim Savage was the absolute and despotic ruler over thousands of Indians ... and was by them designated in their Spanish vernacular *El Rey Guero*—the blonde king."

As Savage amassed a small fortune, he grew increasingly flamboyant. His Indian workers, meanwhile, grew increasingly unhappy as they realized he was growing rich at their expense. On a trip to San Francisco with Indian leader José Juarez, Savage visited a gambling hall, jumped up on a table, and bet his weight in gold on a playing card. In an instant he lost $35,000. He paid the debt with money given to him by Indians to purchase supplies. Juarez, outraged, berated Savage in the street. Savage responded by knocking Juarez to the ground.

Word of Savage's exploits quickly spread among his Indian workers, and Savage returned home to a flurry of discontent. With the situation spiraling out of control, Savage called several Indian leaders together. Addressing them in their native tongue, Savage explained that, "If war is made and the white men are aroused to anger, every Indian engaged in war will be killed."

Juarez, still fuming, stated that white men in faraway cities would not help miners fight Indians. But even if they did, "we will go to the mountains. If they follow, they cannot find us. Our country is now overrun with white people; we must fight to protect ourselves."

THE MARIPOSA BATTALION

N DECEMBER OF 1851, two of Savage's trading posts were raided by angry Indians. Fearful of reprisal, hundreds of Savage's Indian workers fled to the mountains. In response, Savage assembled a 200-man militia called the Mariposa Battalion, with Savage serving as commander.

Before the Battalion could take action, however, federal Indian commissioners arrived and demanded a halt to all hostile activities. Hoping for a diplomatic solution, the commissioners tried to negotiate peace treaties with local tribes. In exchange for leaving the mountains, most "hostile" tribes accepted government land in the Central Valley. But the Ahwahneechee refused. White men had yet to enter Yosemite Valley, and the Ahwahneechee had no interest in leaving their homeland. A stalemate ensued. The Indian commissioners gave the Indians eight days to leave the mountains, but the Indians stood their ground. With no solution at hand, the Mariposa Battalion was sent to Yosemite Valley.

At the time, the Ahwahneechee were led by a powerful chief named Tenaya, who had only recently led his people back to Yosemite. Several decades earlier a terrible plague had swept through the mountains, and Yosemite Valley was abandoned. The survivors, including Tenaya's father, fled to the desert at the eastern base of the Sierra to live with the Mono Indians. Tenaya's father took a Mono wife, and Tenaya was raised among her people, listening to stories of the old days in Yosemite Valley. When Tenaya was a young man, an old shaman urged him to leave the desert and reestablish his people in the mountains. Sometime around 1821, Tenaya returned to Yosemite Valley with 200 followers.

Now, having recently reclaimed their homeland, the Ahwahneechee were confronted with a new threat. As the Mariposa Battalion approached Yosemite Valley, Tenaya headed down to meet with Savage. Tenaya asked why the Indians were being taken from their homeland. Savage explained that the white man would give the Indians everything they needed, including protection.

"We have all we need," Tenaya responded, "we do not want anything from white men … let us remain in the mountains where we were born." Savage was unmoved by the chief's argument. If a treaty is not signed, Savage told Tenaya, "your whole tribe will be destroyed; not one of them will be left alive."

Torn between expulsion and war, Tenaya reluctantly surrendered. A few days later roughly 70 Ahwahneechee trudged out of the mountains through deep snow. But Savage believed many Indians remained hiding in the mountains, so he continued on to Yosemite Valley with roughly 60 Battalion members.

On March 27, 1851 the soldiers reached an overlook with breathtaking views of Yosemite Valley. The light was soft and a fine mist swirled over the trees. One man in the party, Dr. Lafayette Bunnell, was moved to tears by the scenery. Savage thought Bunnell foolish and ordered him to move on. Descending towards Bridalveil Fall, they became the first white men to enter Yosemite Valley.

The next day the men searched the Valley but found only an abandoned Ahwahneechee village. The remaining Indians had fled to higher elevations, and the Battalion, running low on supplies, was forced to turn around. Making matters worse, Tenaya and the other captive Indians somehow managed to escape in the middle of the night. To Savage the expedition was a failure. But Bunnell would later write that, "We had discovered, named, and partially explored, one of the most remarkable ... geographical wonders of the world."

A few weeks later a second expedition was sent to Yosemite Valley, and the Indians were rounded up and marched to the reservation at gunpoint. But life on the reservation was miserable. Tenaya pleaded with his captives to return to Yosemite, and finally he was granted permission to leave. The rest of the tribe quietly followed Tenaya, and no effort was made to bring them back.

Then, in 1852, a group of miners wandered into Yosemite Valley to pan for gold. A skirmish broke out that left two miners dead, and another militia was promptly dispatched to Yosemite. Five Indians were shot and several more were hung from oak trees, but Tenaya, certain that the hostility was not over, ordered his people to cross the Sierras and take shelter with the Mono tribe.

The following year Tenaya led his people back to Yosemite Valley. According to one story, later that fall a group of young Ahwahneechee stole horses from the Mono without Tenaya's permission. The Mono sent a war party to Yosemite Valley in response, and in the skirmish that followed Tenaya was stoned to death. Many young Ahwahneechee were also killed, and the women and children were taken captive by the Mono and marched back over the Sierra. Only a handful of elderly Ahwahneechee were allowed to remain in Yosemite Valley. From that point forward, traditional Ahwahneechee life would never be the same.

GRIZZLY ADAMS

In 1849 a bankrupt Massachusetts shoemaker named James Adams headed to California to try his luck in the Gold Rush. After making and losing several fortunes, Adams grew despondent. "I abandoned all my schemes for wealth," he wrote, " and took the road towards the wildest and most unfrequented parts of the Sierra Nevada, resolved to make the wilderness my home, and wild beasts my companions." In 1856 Adams moved to San Francisco and opened The Mountaineer Museum, which featured elk, eagles, vultures, wildcats, mountain lions, and trained grizzlies that performed tricks. Holding court was Adams himself, dressed in fringed buckskin, moccasins, and a deerskin hat. The museum was a hit, and Adams, who had a knack for publicity, was often seen walking the streets of downtown San Francisco with his grizzlies in tow. His star attraction, Samson, a 1,500 pound grizzly captured in Yosemite, became the model for California's official state flag.

ARTISTS & TOURISTS

A T FIRST, MOST Californians knew nothing of the discovery of Yosemite Valley by the Mariposa Battalion. The foothills were still filled with gold, and most miners could think of little else. Then, in 1855, a journalist named James Hutchings came across a printed account of the Battalion's expedition. He found himself stunned. The discovery of a thousand foot waterfall—*six times* higher than world-famous Niagara Falls—was extraordinary news, and it had yet to be widely reported. Hutchings, who was in the midst of launching an illustrated monthly magazine, immediately set off for the mysterious valley.

Hutchings arrived in Yosemite Valley in June with three companions and two Indian guides. The group spent five days exploring the Valley, taking notes, sketching illustrations, and basking in the scenery. Hutchings was beside himself. The springtime glory of the Valley far exceeded his expectations—the waterfall he had read about was over *two thousand* feet high—and shortly thereafter he wrote a glowing article for a Mariposa newspaper describing the "luxurious scenic banqueting." By the end of the summer, over 40 people had visited Yosemite Valley.

The following year two enterprising miners opened a 50-mile horse trail to Yosemite, charging $2 per horseback rider. The multi-day ride, which involved steep climbs and sheer drop-offs, was enough to deter most visitors, but a few dozen adventurous souls were willing to brave the hardship to witness the scenery firsthand. The first hotel in Yosemite Valley opened for business in 1857, followed by an even larger hotel two years later. Both structures consisted of dirt floors, rooms separated by hanging sheets, and windows with no panes. But by all accounts the hospitality made up for the rustic accommodations.

Halfway along the trail to Yosemite was a large meadow called Wawona, and Galen Clark, one of the first visitors to Yosemite Valley, took up residence there in 1856. Shortly after building an inn for overnight guests, Clark discovered a nearby grove of giant sequoias. Before long, the Big Trees had become a must-see destination on par with Yosemite Valley.

James Hutchings

As news of Yosemite's extraordinary scenery rippled through California society, more and more people stopped by for a look. Artists were among the earliest arrivals, and their photos, paintings, and illustrations further fueled public curiosity. In 1861 the influential Reverend Thomas Starr King visited Yosemite Valley, and upon returning to San Francisco he preached its wonders from his pulpit and wrote compelling articles that reached a national

Galen Clark

IN 1855 GALEN CLARK visited Yosemite Valley as a member of the second tourist party. Several months later he developed serious lung problems, and he was told that he only had a short time to live. In 1857 Clark, who was then 42, moved to present-day Wawona. "I went to the mountains," he wrote, "to take my chances of dying or growing better which I thought were about even." Shortly thereafter he completely recovered, and Clark spent most of the next 53 years in the park.

Born in Canada in 1814, Clark was a polite, sickly child who achieved little success as a young man. In 1853 he was broke and living in New York City when he saw an exhibition displaying gold dust from the Sierra Nevada. Enchanted, he immediately set sail for California, ending up as a miner in Mariposa County. After developing lung problems he claimed 160 acres in Wawona and built a cabin in the meadow. After regaining his health, Clark discovered the nearby Mariposa grove of giant sequoias, which he wasted no time in publicizing. Soon he was hosting many guests in his small hotel. The influential Thomas Starr King called Clark, "one of the best informed men, one of the very best guides, I ever met in California or any other wilderness. He is a fine-looking, stalwart old grizzly hunter and miner of the 49 days." Another guest described him as, "hand-some, thoughtful, interesting, and slovenly." Although universally beloved, Clark had many unusual habits. He frequently went barefoot, claiming that shoes and boots were, "cruel and silly instruments of torture, at once uncivilized, inhuman, and unnecessary." And while hiking Clark intentionally breathed through his nose, believing that, "As the air rushes through the nostrils on its way to inflate the lungs, the brain attracts and inhales electricity from it."

When the Yosemite Grant was created in 1864, Clark became the first "Guardian" of Yosemite (a position comparable to park superintendent today). Later Clark became an early member of the Sierra Club. John Muir described him as "the best mountaineer I ever met, and one of the kindest and most ami-able of all my mountain friends." In 1904, when Clark was 90 years old, another friend noted that "notwithstanding his great age, he easily makes long trips on foot and horseback which would fatigue a much younger man." In 1910 he died at the age of 96. By that point Mount Clark and the Clark Range in Yosemite had been named in his honor.

audience. That same year Hutchings published *Scenes of Wonder and Curiosity in California*, an illustrated book that lavished praise upon Yosemite. To Hutchings, who would soon purchase a hotel in the Valley, Yosemite was an underexploited scenic gold mine. But as hoteliers and settlers snatched up plots of land, some visitors grew concerned at the pace of unchecked development.

In early 1864 a group of influential citizens approached California Senator John Conness with a novel idea. The group believed that a location as unique as Yosemite should belong to the public, as opposed to a handful of private land-owners, and they urged the creation of a state-owned land trust to preserve Yosemite for the enjoyment of future generations. Spearheading the effort was Israel Raymond, a wealthy San Francisco businessman. In 1864 Raymond urged Conness to transfer Yosemite and the Mariposa Grove from the federal govern-ment to the State of California "for public use and recreation."

Conness liked the idea, and in 1864 he presented a bill to Congress that passed with little opposition. On June 30, 1864, in the midst of the Civil War, President Abraham Lincoln signed the Yosemite Grant into law.

Although few realized it at the time, the bill was a stunning achievement. Never before in history had a piece of land been set aside simply for scenic beauty. It was an idea that would turn out to be highly contagious.

PAINTERS & PHOTOGRAPHERS

EADWARD MUYBRIDGE

EADWEARD MUYBRIDGE WAS not the first photographer to visit Yosemite, but he was the first photographer to take a romantic approach, composing his shots like landscape paintings and adding embellished details like clouds as he saw fit. Following his first visit to Yosemite, Muybridge (who had a flair for drama) secretly adopted the pseudonym "Helios." He then exhibited Helios' Yosemite photographs in a San Francisco gallery and then handed out brochures commenting on the "anonymous" artist's supreme talents. The response was overwhelming: people *loved* the mystery photographer's painterly approach. When it was revealed that Muybridge was Helios, critics were appalled, but the public reacted with a collective shrug and Muybridge's career continued to thrive.

In 1871, at the age of 41, Muybridge married his 21-year-old photography assistant. A few years later, convinced his wife was cheating on him, Muybridge tracked down her supposed lover to a home near Calistoga and shot him through the heart. He then apologized to several women present, calmly sat down in the parlor, and began reading a newspaper. He was ultimately acquitted of the murder on the grounds of "justifiable homicide." Later Muybridge abandoned landscape photography to focus on photographic motion studies, which laid the groundwork for the invention of motion pictures a decade later.

ALBERT BIERSTADT

MANY PAINTERS VISITED Yosemite in the mid-1800s, but none derived as much fame or success from the scenery as Albert Bierstadt. When Bierstadt arrived in Yosemite in 1863, landscape painting exhibitions drew block-buster crowds in major American cities, offering the public a rare glimpse of remote, exotic places that few people had the time or the money to visit. Landscape artists were treated like rock stars, and Bierstadt's massive, melodramatic landscapes were among the most popular. A master of self-promotion, he displayed his works as if they were performances: charging admission, unveiling them behind velvet curtains, lighting them dramatically, and even recommending that viewers scan them through binoculars to heighten the visual effect.

His first monumental Yosemite painting, *Looking Down Yosemite Valley, California* (above), measured 40 square feet and was unveiled to the public in 1865. The painting established Bierstadt as America's top landscape artist, and the giant canvas promptly toured several major cities. In 1867 a wealthy financier commissioned a massive 140 square-foot Yosemite painting for the astounding sum of $25,000. When that painting, *The Domes of Yosemite*, was unveiled to the public, it caused a firestorm of criticism. Some considered it Bierstadt's finest work, but others accused Bierstadt of vulgar exaggeration. The scenery was simply *too* perfect. When Mark Twain viewed the canvas he joked that it was, " considerably more beautiful than the original," describing it as, " more the atmosphere of Kingdom-Come than of California." Although some critics scoffed, Bierstadt remained one of the most popular and influential landscape artists of the 19th century.

John Muir

Of all the great artists and thinkers Yosemite has nurtured, none has been more celebrated, more influential, and more romanticized than John Muir. His eloquent nature writing helped inspire the modern environmental movement, and his tireless efforts were vital to the establishment of Yosemite National Park.

Born in Scotland in 1838, Muir moved to Wisconsin with his parents when he was a child. Later Muir enrolled at the University of Wisconsin, but he quit before graduation to enter what he called "the University of the Wilderness." In 1867, after recovering from an accident that nearly left him blind, Muir embarked on a 1,000 mile walk to Florida.

From Florida Muir set sail for California, arriving in San Francisco in 1868. He immediately set out on a six-week walk to Yosemite. Spellbound by Yosemite's scenery—"every feature glowing, radiating beauty that pours into our flesh and bones like heat rays from fire"—Muir found employment the following summer as a sheepherder in the Sierra Nevada. Wandering among the alpine meadows with a St. Bernard, Muir rejoiced in the mountain wilderness. In his free time he studied plants and climbed the granite peaks. "This June seems the greatest of all the months of my life," he wrote. By the end of the summer, Muir had developed a passion for the Sierra Nevada, which he christened the "Range of Light."

The following summer Muir worked at a sawmill in Yosemite Valley, and for the next several years he rambled about the Sierra Nevada, meticulously studying the natural landscape and taking copious notes. He often wandered for days in the wilderness, carrying nothing more than a blanket, a notebook, some tea and dry bread. Around this time Muir began writing popular nature articles for newspapers and magazines.

In 1880 Muir married the daughter of a wealthy California fruit farmer. Settling down for the first time in his life, he spent the next several years working the farm and raising two daughters. But domestic life wore on Muir, and in 1888 his wife sold parcels of the family estate to allow

"Climb the mountains and get their good tidings. Nature's peace will flow through you as the sunshine into the trees. The winds will blow their freshness into you, and the storms their energy, while cares will drop off like autumn leaves."

Muir to focus on his wilderness studies. Shortly there-
after he teamed up with the influential editor Robert
Underwood Johnston to spearhead the creation of
Yosemite National Park.

In 1892 Muir co-founded the Sierra Club and became
its first president. Muir's first book, *The Mountains of
California*, was published two years later when he was
56 years old. The book was an instant success, and several books followed that are now considered nature classics.
"Strange is it not that a tramp and vagabond should meet such
a fate," he wrote, "I never intended to write or lecture or seek fame in any way,
I now write a great deal, and am well known." In 1903 Muir embarked on a year-
long, round-the-world journey, then spent the final decade of his life fighting to
stop the damming of Hetch Hetchy Valley in Yosemite—a battle that was lost
in 1913. Several months later, Muir died of pneumonia.

Although Muir is often portrayed as a contemplative mountain poet, his
younger days were characterized by brash, youthful machismo. His testosterone-
fueled exploits included climbing mountains in winter, riding out storms in
trees, and generally risking life and limb. At one point he shimmied to the lip of
Yosemite Falls just to check out the view. Such death-defying exploits profoundly
influenced his writing. Whereas earlier environmental thinkers such as Emerson
and Thoreau took leisurely strolls through the woods, Muir threw himself into
nature with the physical vigor of an athlete.

Muir's eloquent, adventurous writing continues to resonate with a huge audience today. His extraordinary ability to communicate the importance of wilderness preservation has influenced generations of prominent thinkers, and his once
local celebrity has morphed into environmental superstardom. Today his cult of
personality can be seen on T-shirts, posters, and bumper stickers that read "Muir
Power to You!"

Muir's sketch of the High Sierra

BECOMING A NATIONAL PARK

YOSEMITE VALLEY WAS officially protected in 1864, but under lax state management the Valley developed into a cluttered series of roads, hotels, cabins, and pastures for cattle. Land was tilled and irrigated to provide food for residents, and a timber mill provided wood for construction and heating.

Meanwhile sheepherders marched thousands of sheep through the mountains above Yosemite to graze in the pristine meadows. The combined munching, chomping, and trampling left the delicate meadows in disarray. During John Muir's first summer as a sheepherder in the High Sierra, he witnessed this destruction first hand. "To let sheep trample so divinely fine a place seems barbarous," he wrote. Later he put the destruction in even sharper terms, referring to sheep as "hooved locusts."

In 1889 Muir went camping with Robert Underwood Johnson, editor of nationally influential *Century* magazine. Around a campfire in Tuolumne Meadows the two men discussed the beauty of Yosemite and the Sierra Nevada and the threat that grazing and development posed. In 1872 Yellowstone had become the nation's first national park, and though Yosemite Valley and the Mariposa Grove were officially protected by the state (on paper, at least), Muir and Johnson believed the mountains surrounding Yosemite—and notably the watershed that fed Yosemite Valley—also deserved national park status.

Returning from their camping trip, the two men embarked on a savvy media campaign to rally public support for their cause. Muir wrote articles for *Century* extolling the beauty of Yosemite and the threats that it faced, and both men stumped for the cause in speeches around the country. Their tireless efforts led to the creation of Yosemite National Park on October 1, 1890. To protect the nearly one million acres of pristine Sierra Nevada wilderness, units of the Army Calvary were dispatched to Wawona. In the summer the Calvary patrolled the mountains on horseback, driving out sheepherders, cattlemen, and hunters.

Still, the Yosemite Grant (Yosemite Valley and the Mariposa Grove) remained under state jurisdiction, and Muir firmly believed they needed to be transferred to Yosemite National Park to be truly protected. In 1895 he described Yosemite Valley as, "downtrodden, frowsy, and like an abandoned backwoods pasture. It looks ten times worse now than ... seven years ago. Most of the level meadow floor of the Valley is fenced with barbed and unbarbed wire and about three hundred head of horses are turned loose every night to feed and trample the flora out of existence ... As long as the management is in the hands of eight politicians appointed by the ever-changing Governor of California, there is but little hope."

Robert Underwood Johnson

Teddy Roosevelt & John Muir

Salvation came in the form of President Theodore Roosevelt, who visited Yosemite Valley in 1903. Although Roosevelt requested no fanfare or celebrations to herald his arrival, Valley residents planned a lavish banquet attended by the Governor of California and followed by an expensive fireworks display. Dismayed, the President asked Muir to show him the *real* Yosemite, and the two men quietly slipped into the backcountry for several nights of camping. Around a roaring campfire Roosevelt and Muir talked late into the night, slept in the brisk open air, and woke up to a dusting of snow. "I've had the time of my life," Roosevelt later told reporters, "Just think of where I was last night. Up there amid the pines and the silver firs, in the Sierran solitude, and without a tent. I passed one of the most pleasant nights of my life."

With Roosevelt's support firmly in place, Muir and the Sierra Club lobbied hard to transfer the Yosemite Grant to the National Park Service. After a bitter fight in the California legislature, the bill was passed and sent to Washington. Again Muir stepped into action, cajoling Congressmen and pulling strings to secure the necessary votes. Finally, on June 11, 1906, President Roosevelt signed the bill into law. Elated, Muir wrote to his old friend Robert Underwood Johnson. "Sound the loud trimble and let every Yosemite tree and stream rejoice ... The fight you planned by that famous Tuolumne camp-fire seventeen years ago is at last fairly, gloriously won, every enemy down." In fact, a new fight was looming on the horizon.

California Grizzlies

CALIFORNIA REPUBLIC

Prior to European contact, grizzly bears were abundant throughout California. Highly adaptable, their range covered most of the state excluding the High Sierra and the eastern deserts. Estimates of California's historic grizzly population range as high as 10,000. "It was not uncommon to see thirty to forty a day," noted one man in the Sacramento Valley in 1841. By 1922, however, not a single grizzly bear remained in the state.

Grizzlies are the largest and most powerful bear in North America, distinguished by a large, muscular hump over the shoulders that powers explosive digging ability. Weighing up to 1,500 pounds, they require vast quantities of food on a daily basis. Although grizzlies are omnivores—eating plants, animals, insects, and just about anything else—when missions and ranches were established in California in the 1600s, many grizzlies found it easier to kill cattle and other livestock than to hunt wild food. Before long, bored Mexican ranchers were capturing live grizzlies for bull-and-bear fights, where the two animals, tethered together, fought to the death. The grizzly generally won the first round, at which point the ranchers tied up a new bull. Such spectacles supposedly influenced New York newspaper editor Horace Greeley to coin the terms Bull Market and Bear Market, because the bull—or more accurately *bulls*—always won.

During the Bear Flag Revolt of 1846, Americans revolted against Mexican authorities in California. After a swift victory, the Americans raised a new flag that featured a grizzly bear. The flag had a brief career, however, flying less than a month before it was replaced by the stars and stripes. A modified version of the Bear Flag (above) was adopted as California's official state flag in 1911. By that point, however, few grizzly bears remained. That last known Yosemite grizzly was shot in 1895, and the last known California grizzly was killed in Sequoia National Forest in 1922.

THE BATTLE FOR HETCH HETCHY

SIX WEEKS BEFORE Yosemite Valley officially became part of Yosemite National Park, San Francisco lay in ruins. On April 18, 1906 a massive earthquake shook the town, demolishing buildings and other man-made structures. Most of the damage occurred after the earthquake, however, when a massive fire raced through town and incinerated over 500 city blocks. With hopelessly limited access to water, residents could do little but watch their glorious city burn. In the end, more than half of the city's 400,000 citizens were left homeless and roughly 3,000 people died. A century later, it remained the largest loss of life due to a natural disaster in California's history.

In spite of the catastrophe, the human spirit prevailed and the citizens of San Francisco rallied to rebuild their home. It was a remarkable effort, but a vexing problem remained: San Francisco, which is situated at the tip of a small peninsula, has no natural water supply.

During the boom years of the Gold Rush, fresh water was ferried to San Francisco on schooners, poured into large casks, and hauled up the city's steep streets by weary horses and mules. (Such sorry sights inspired Andrew Hallidie, an animal lover, to invent the cable car.) Later a Roman-style aqueduct—the first in America—delivered water from a large creek 20 miles distant.

By 1906, however, this limited water supply was completely inadequate for the city's booming population—a fact that became painfully clear in the wake of the earthquake. As civic leaders struggled to build a new and improved San Francisco, one of their top priorities was securing a large, reliable source of water. And one of the most promising sites for a new reservoir was Hetch Hetchy Valley in Yosemite National Park.

Lying just 25 miles north of Yosemite Valley, Hetch Hetchy was considered by many to be Yosemite's sister valley. It too was surrounded by massive granite cliffs and thundering waterfalls, and though smaller it was similarly impressive. The famous geologist Josiah Whitney described Hetch Hetchy as "almost an exact counterpart of the Yosemite Valley [although] not on quite as grand a scale as that valley. But if there were no Yosemite, the Hetch Hetchy would be fairly entitled to a worldwide fame."

In 1871 John Muir called Hetch Hetchy "one of Nature's rarest and most precious mountain temples." When talk of a potential dam in Hetch Hetchy first surfaced, Muir readied himself for battle. Other rivers could quench San Francisco's thirst, and Muir was determined to protect the beautiful valley where he had spent many happy days and nights. It was illegal, he pointed out, to build a dam in a national park. Dam proponents responded by introducing legislation to remove that technicality. When the legal sleight-of-hand was blocked, dam proponents presented the conflict as all of San Francisco against a few wealthy hiking enthusiasts from the Sierra Club.

Following the earthquake, Muir was up against even longer odds. The emotionally and financially shattered residents of San Francisco were desperate for peace of mind, and feasibility studies indicated that Hetch Hetchy was the most cost-effective source of water for the devastated city. Again the cry went up to dam Hetch Hetchy, but Muir and the Sierra Club fought back.

Insults were hurled back and forth, and soon the local battle spilled over into the national arena. One of the most prominent supporters of the dam was Gifford Pinchot, the brilliant young head of the U.S. Forest Service who preached conservation over preservation, so-called "wise use" that sought to sustainably protect natural resources while utilizing them for the greatest possible good. His argument for the dam at Hetch Hetchy struck a similar chord. "The injury," he wrote, "by substituting a lake for the present swampy floor of the valley ... is altogether unimportant compared with the benefits to be derived from its use as a reservoir." Visitation numbers seemed to support this—rarely did more than 200 people visit the swampy, mosquito-infested valley each summer.

Both Muir and Pinchot were devout proponents of wilderness protection, but their ideologies shared little else in common. Pinchot believed wild resources, used sustainably, should be put to the greatest possible good, while Muir, ever the romantic, wanted strict preservation for recreational use only. "Dam Hetch Hetchy! As well dam for water-tanks the people's cathedrals and churches," wrote Muir, "for no holier temple has ever been consecrated by the heart of man." It was classic Muir, wrapping nature preservation in condemnatory, religious rhetoric. In a lighter moment Muir confided to a friend, "How this business Hetch-hetchs one's time. It won't even let me sleep."

As the two sides traded barbs, the fight dragged on for many years. Using his considerable influence, Muir enlisted support from many powerful friends, including Presidents Roosevelt and Taft, who blocked any legislation favoring the dam. When Woodrow Wilson won the presidential election in 1912, however, he sided with proponents of the dam.

In less than a year the Raker Act, which authorized the damming of Hetch Hetchy, passed both houses of Congress and was signed into law. John Raker, the bill's main proponent, claimed the reservoir would be the "highest form of conservation," making the valley more accessible and useful for recreation. "As to damning the dammers they are damned already and buried beneath a roaring flood of lies," wrote Muir, who died a year later at the age of 76.

The battle over Hetch Hetchy was a milestone in American politics. It was the first national debate to pit the necessities of urban growth against environmental preservation. As such it set the tone for many future battles. The lessons learned by both sides were analyzed, critiqued, and refined to a high art. In the 1950s, dam builders flooded scenic Glen Canyon in southern Utah. A few years later, the Sierra Club blocked two proposed dams in Grand Canyon using a brilliant PR campaign that paraphrased John Muir. Today, the ongoing debate of wise-use versus strict preservation continues to rage.

Hetch Hetchy Valley, pre-dam

"As in Yosemite, the sublime rocks of its walls seem to glow with life, whether leaning back in repose or standing erect in thoughtful attitudes, giving welcome to storms and calms alike, their brows in the sky, their feet set in groves and gay flowers, while birds, bees, and butterflies help the river and waterfalls to stir all the air into music—things frail and fleeting and types of permanence meeting here and blending, just as they do in Yosemite, to draw her lovers into close and confiding communion."

THE NATIONAL PARK SERVICE

T HROUGHOUT THE HETCH HETCHY debate, the U.S. Calvary dutifully looked after Yosemite. Although several national parks had been established by the turn of the century, the National Park Service had not yet been established, so Yosemite's operation fell to the military. After decades of exemplary service, the cavalry was replaced by a civilian force in 1914.

That same year a wealthy industrialist named Stephen Mather wrote a letter of complaint to Secretary of the Interior Franklin K. Lane. Mather, who made his fortune mining borax in Death Valley, was frustrated with the way America's national parks were being managed, and he demanded that something be done. Lane's response: "If you don't like the way the national parks are being run, come on down to Washington and run them yourself." Mather did just that. For the next 14 years, Mather shaped a strong vision for America's national parks.

Mather's first step was to establish a government agency to oversee the national parks. On August 25, 1916, President Woodrow Wilson signed the Organic Act, which established the National Park Service. Mather was named director of the new agency, and his first priority was to boost park visitation. Mather realized that more visitors would translate to greater public support, which the fledgling agency desperately needed to justify its existence and ensure its future survival.

To accommodate automobiles, which were becoming increasingly popular in Yosemite, Mather secured funds to replace roads designed for horses with improved automobile roads. The result was predictable: visitation boomed. In 1915 roughly 15,000 people visited the park. Five years later, that number jumped to nearly 69,000.

To accommodate the new visitors, Mather championed the construction of new hotels. "Scenery," wrote Mather, "is a hollow enjoyment to a tourist who sets out in the morning after an indigestible breakfast and a fitful sleep on an impossible bed." The park soon offered a wide range of lodging options, but the crown jewel was the sumptuous Ahwahnee Hotel—Mather's masterpiece for his favorite national park.

Despite the physical improvements, many basic problems remained. Yosemite was still riddled with "inholdings" (privately owned parcels of land purchased before the creation of the park) that were vulnerable to mining, logging, and development. In 1930 John D. Rockefeller, Jr. put up half the money needed to purchase 15,000 acres of private land; the rest was provided by Congress.

Under Mather's watchful eye Yosemite Valley became a recreational wonderland that lured thousands of tourists each year. Decades later, with annual visitation well into the millions, some would question the wisdom of this policy. But at the time Mather's policies were essential to ensure the long-term survival of the National Park Service.

Ansel Adams

Many artists have been inspired by Yosemite, but none will ever be as singularly identified with the park as Ansel Adams. His stunning black and white photographs elevated landscape photography to lofty new heights, and his visual genius has rarely been eclipsed.

Born to an upper-class San Francisco family, Adams was an odd, hyperactive child. A talented musician, he dreamed of becoming a concert pianist, but while recovering from an illness he discovered a copy of James Hutchings' book *In the Heart of the Sierras*. Captivated by the photographs, Adams begged his family to visit Yosemite. In 1916 his wish was fulfilled, and upon entering Yosemite Valley Ansel's loving father presented him with a fateful gift: a small Kodak camera.

At 17 Adams joined the Sierra Club and participated in many High Sierra camping trips. But he soon became frustrated with his simple camera, which took drab pictures that failed to convey the powerful emotions he felt. To remedy the situation, Adams immersed himself in advanced photography.

Over the next two decades Adams produced hundreds of dazzling landscapes distinguished by bold, lush tonality. Assorted darkroom techniques allowed him to heighten the drama, infusing wilderness scenes with personal emotion—what he *felt* in addition to what he saw. "When I'm ready to make a photograph," he said, "I see in my mind's eye something that is not literally there ... I'm interested in expressing something which is built up from within, rather than extracted from without."

Adams rigorous work ethic and finely-tuned creative instincts catapulted him to the top of the art world. Although his best work was done in his 20s and 30s—sometimes working at an unsustainable manic pace—in later life Adams eagerly adopted the role of elder statesmen. He campaigned on behalf of the American Wilderness and endeared himself to the public with his enthusiasm and charm. Unlike many landscape photographers Adams was a gregarious bon vivant. He always relished a party, frequently holding forth at the piano while strong drinks were poured late into the night.

Adams served on the board of the Sierra Club for 37 years, and throughout the 20th century his wildly popular photographs inspired millions of Americans to embrace environmentalism. In 1940 his photographs helped establish Kings Canyon National Park. By 1980, when he was awarded the Presidential Medal of Freedom, he had become that rarest of breeds: an internationally famous living artist. Following his death in 1984, both the Ansel Adams Wilderness and Mount Ansel Adams in Yosemite were named in his honor.

Mount Ansel Adams

YOSEMITE ROCK STARS

BY THE DAWN of the 20th century, most famous peaks in Yosemite had been summited. A few first ascents were made by the California Geological Survey, which mapped the entire Sierra Nevada in the 1860s, but the Survey labeled several rugged peaks "inaccessible." Predictably, such declarations only whetted the appetites of hardy adventurers, and soon every notable peak in Yosemite had been conquered.

In 1931 Robert Underhill visited the Sierra Nevada and introduced mountaineering techniques from Europe. The Europeans had pioneered mountain climbing in the 1800s, and they remained the sport's preeminent practitioners for decades. Underhill helped the Americans play catch up, blazing difficult new routes up previously conquered peaks. But following WWII and the introduction of nylon ropes, the sport of climbing forever changed.

Prior to nylon, ropes were made out of hemp that snapped under sudden, intense pressure—a taught rope caused by a falling climber, say. As a result, falling was anathema, a fatal mistake avoided at all costs. But the new, virtually unbreakable nylon ropes allowed climbers to tackle previously unthinkable challenges. Confident that the new ropes would protect them, climbers attempted risky new moves that often caused them to fall. In the brave new post-nylon world, falling was suddenly acceptable. Through dedicated trial and error, climbers perfected complex gravity-defying moves and were soon scampering up vertical faces where no rational human belonged.

Armed with impressive new skills, climbers sought out bigger and bigger walls. And no place on Earth had more fantastically big walls in a more gloriously accessible location than Yosemite. In the 1940s and 50s a motley collection of climbing personalities descended on the park to put their skills to the test. Among the new arrivals was a 47-year-old Swiss ironworker named John Salathé, who pioneered an important new piece of climbing equipment: the steel piton. This strong metal spike, fashioned with an eye-hole at one end, could be hammered into cracks to provide a safe, secure anchor for ropes.

Although pitons already existed in Europe, they were made with soft, malleable iron that often buckled in Yosemite's hard granite cracks. Salathé's steel pitons, by contrast, held strong and could be reused, which meant carrying much less equipment on big climbs. Salathé then unleashed another revolutionary concept in Yosemite: the multi-day climb. After climbing all day, Salathé spent the night strapped to the face of the rock. No longer constrained by equipment or daylight, climbers could rise as high as their bodies would take them.

Yosemite's pioneering "granite astronauts" soon conquered the Valley's most storied landmarks. Salathé kicked off the trend by completing the first multi-day first ascent of Lost Arrow Spire (1947) and 1,500-foot Sentinel Rock (1950). In

Lost Arrow Spire

1957 Royal Robbins, Jerry Gallwas, and Mike Sherrick climbed the vertical 2,000-foot Northwest Face of Half Dome in five days. The trio was graciously greeted at the top by Warren Harding, Robbins' rival, but the jealous Harding quickly made it his personal mission to bag the granddaddy of them all: El Capitan.

In 1958 Harding and two friends (Wayne Merry and George Whitmore) reached the top of El Capitan using "siege tactics"—setting ropes higher and higher and rappelling down for rest and supplies. It took the team 45 days spread over 18 months. Robbins considered such tactics poor form, and in 1960 he assembled a group to retrace Harding's route in a committed seven-day push.

Over the next decade many future climbing legends came to Yosemite Valley and left their mark, establishing dozens of challenging new routes. By the early 1970s, however, the popularity of rock climbing was exploding, and the once-minimal damage caused by pitons began to raise concerns. Hammering pitons into and out of cracks distorted the rock, leaving behind a rounded scar. Many popular routes were riddled with piton marks, and the damage was compounding each year.

In 1973 three climbers—Galen Rowell, Dennis Henneck, and Doug Robinson—climbed the Northwest Face of Half Dome using radical "clean" gear that left no trace. Rather than hammering in pitons, they wedged bolt-sized pieces of aluminum into hairline cracks. The aluminum pieces were fashioned in a wide variety of shapes and sizes to accommodate whatever cracks the trio encountered, and they could easily be un-wedged without leaving a scar. *National Geographic* devoted a cover story to their endeavor, and soon chocks and nuts (as the aluminum pieces came to be called) were commercially available. A new era of rock conservation had begun. Any half decent climber could hammer their way to the top of a route, the new climbing philosophers preached, but it was better to rise to meet the challenge of the rock than to lower the difficulty of the climb to compensate for personal weakness.

Then, in the 1980s, American climbers at other popular climbing destinations began drilling many small permanent bolts into rock faces to standardize climbs. This allowed climbers to focus less on equipment and more on pure athletic ability. Although bolts were often spaced widely apart to retain the challenge of the rock, this new style of climbing, called sport climbing, met with vehement resistance in Yosemite. Purists deplored the "excessive" bolt-drilling, and many verbal—and sometimes physical—confrontations ensued. "Sport Climbing Is Neither" mocked a popular bumper sticker. Gradually, however, the practice was grudgingly accepted, and an uneasy truce has remained in place ever since.

Today roughly five percent of Yosemite visitors—nearly 200,000 people—identify themselves as rock climbers. Young climbers come to follow in the footsteps of living legends, while old timers climb well into their 60s, 70s, and even 80s. Today, as always, Yosemite Valley lies at the heart of American rock climbing. Its history, legends, and personalities have influenced several generations of climbers, and they will continue to shape the sport's culture for years to come.

YOSEMITE TODAY

ODAY YOSEMITE IS one of America's most popular national parks. Its world-class scenery lures visitors from around the globe, but the park's immense popularity now poses significant challenges. In 1855, the first year of tourism in Yosemite, 42 people visited the Valley. A century later annual visitation topped one million, and the numbers kept on climbing—two million in 1967, three million in 1987, four million in 1994. In Yosemite Valley, where most visitation is concentrated, peak-season traffic jams and long lines became as much a part of the scenery as cliffs and waterfalls. To alleviate congestion, the park service established one-way roads, initiated a free shuttle service, and reduced the number of hotel rooms and campsites.

Managing a park as large and popular as Yosemite is a complex, difficult job. The National Park Service bears the burden of both protecting the natural resource and providing for the enjoyment of park visitors—two often conflicting goals. In 2000 a general management plan outlined five main priorities for Yosemite: reduce visual intrusion of administrative and commercial services, reduce crowding, reduce traffic congestion, allow natural processes to prevail, and promote visitor understanding through enhanced interpretive programming and educational facilities. Successfully achieving these goals is a challenge. But with a dedicated staff, a passionate public following, and the support of terrific organizations like the Yosemite Association, the Yosemite Institute, and the Yosemite Fund, Yosemite's future looks bright.

YOSEMITE VALLEY

✯ ✯ ✯ ✯ ✯

Introduction 127
Basics 128
Map 132
Sights 134
Hiking 166

YOSEMITE VALLEY

THREE THOUSAND-FOOT CLIFFS. Thundering waterfalls. Sparkling granite domes. Yosemite Valley is without question the most spectacular part of the park. Just seven miles long and less than one mile wide, it's home to four of the world's ten tallest waterfalls and enough heart-pounding scenery to keep you in a perpetual state of awe. Its physical drama and picture perfect layout are almost beyond belief. As John Muir once wrote, it's "as if into this one mountain mansion Nature had gathered her choicest treasures."

How you choose to bask in the scenery is entirely up to you. If you're here to relax, you can spend the day lounging along the banks of the Merced River or ride around the Valley on a narrated tram tour. Those looking for a bit more action can pedal along bicycle paths, hike along the Valley's stunning trails, or sign up for a rock climbing lesson. Free ranger programs are also offered throughout the day, with topics ranging from natural history to photography.

As the belle of the Yosemite ball, the Valley lures millions of visitors each year. At times, this definitely has its drawbacks. Roughly 80 percent of visitors spend their time in Yosemite Valley, and the resulting crowds sometimes create long lines and parking hassles. But no matter how crowded the Valley gets—and on Labor Day, Memorial Day, and the Fourth of July it can get *very* crowded—nothing can take away from the jaw-dropping scenery.

Even if you visit on busy summer weekends, there are still a few tricks to escape the crowds. Tip #1: Head to popular sights in the early morning or late afternoon—you'll avoid the worst of the crowds *and* revel in the gorgeous light. Tip #2: go for a hike—crowds thin out exponentially for every foot that you climb (hyperpopular Mist Trail notwithstanding). Even an easy stroll to Mirror Lake is capable of delivering solitude if you hike beyond the popular sights.

May and June are the best months to visit Yosemite Valley. Over a dozen spectacular waterfalls tumble down from the rim, temperatures are mild, the wildflowers are in bloom, and the dense crowds have yet to arrive. July and August are hot and crowded, but autumn soon brings ideal weather and a glorious display of foliage. Winter is the least popular time to visit, but after a fresh layer of snow Yosemite Valley is dazzling. Peace and quiet descends over the Valley, and lodging bargains abound.

Yosemite Valley
BASICS

GETTING AROUND YOSEMITE VALLEY

Although you can drive throughout much of Yosemite Valley, parking can be a hassle. Fortunately, a free shuttle runs daily from 7am to 10 pm, making frequent stops at hotels, campground, and most major sights in eastern Yosemite Valley. (Some popular stops in eastern Yosemite Valley—Happy Isles, Mirror Lake—are off limits to private vehicles, and can only be reached by shuttle or on foot.) From May through September shuttles run about every 10–15 minutes. In the off-season shuttles run about every 30 minutes. Current shuttle routes and stops are listed in *Yosemite Today*.

The shuttle is great if you're short on energy or time. But the best way to explore Yosemite Valley is on foot or bike, traveling at your own pace and taking plenty of time to soak in the sights. Hikers can follow the easy 13-mile Valley Loop Trail, which circumnavigates the entire floor of Yosemite Valley. Although rundown and confusing at times, much of the path is in good shape and easy to follow. Two popular starting points are Curry Village and Yosemite Lodge. Bicyclists, meanwhile, can enjoy 12 miles of traffic-free bike paths adjacent to main roads in eastern Yosemite Valley.

PARKING

There are two major day-use parking areas in Yosemite Valley. The largest is located just south of the four-way intersection near Yosemite Village. Another parking area is located adjacent to Curry Village.

VISITOR CENTERS AND INFO

The Yosemite Visitor Center (p.134) in Yosemite Village is the largest and most popular visitor center in the Valley. Small information booths are also located at all of the Valley's hotels and campgrounds.

LODGING & CAMPING

See page 36.

ACTIVITIES

FREE RANGER PROGRAMS
A wide range of free ranger programs—nature walks, photography walks, camp-fires, evening programs, etc.— are offered throughout the year. Check *Yosemite Today* for the current schedule.

GUIDED TOURS
Narrated tours are offered throughout the year. A popular two-hour, open-air tram tour (about $20/person) departs several times daily from Yosemite Lodge. Full moon Valley tours are also available. Longer tours depart for Glacier Point and the Mariposa Grove of giant sequoias. Purchase tickets at Yosemite Lodge, Curry Village, or the small kiosk next to the Yosemite Village Store.

ROCK CLIMBING
See page 25.

RIVER RAFTING
Curry Village rents 6-person rafts (about $15/person) in the late spring/early summer for lazy floats down the Merced River (p.31)

BIKING
Bicycles can be rented (about $25/day) at Curry Village and Yosemite Lodge.

DINING

THE AHWAHNEE DINING ROOM
Yosemite's ultimate dining experience. Gourmet food served in the Ahwahnee Hotel's sumptuous wood-beamed dining hall. Breakfast, lunch, and dinner are served. Reservations are required for dinner and recommended for other meals. Formal attire required at dinner. (Expensive; open year-round, 209-372-1489)

CURRY VILLAGE
Curry Village offers several dining options in the spring, summer, and fall. The Pavilion Buffet, located in the large building near the amphitheater, serves all-you-can-eat, buffet-style breakfast and dinner at moderate prices. Nearby there's the gourmet Coffee Corner and the popular Pizza Deck. Around the corner is Curry Taqueria, serving cheap burritos and other Mexican favorites.

DEGNAN'S DELI & CAFE
Serves the best deli sandwiches in the Valley—perfect for a picnic lunch. A small take-out stand adjacent to the deli also serves burgers and fast food. (Inexpensive; open year-round)

DINING (continued)

DEGNAN'S PIZZA LOFT

Serves the best pizza in the Valley, but expect long lines in the summer. Located above Degnan's Deli in Yosemite Village. (Moderate prices, open spring to fall)

THE MOUNTAIN ROOM

This steakhouse-style restaurant features the Valley's second best menu. Located at Yosemite Lodge, it features great views of Yosemite Falls. (Moderately expensive; dinner only; open year-round, 209-372-1274)

THE VILLAGE GRILL

This simple takeout serves burgers, fries, and other fast food favorites for lunch and dinner. Located in Yosemite Village. (Inexpensive; open spring to fall)

YOSEMITE LODGE FOOD COURT

Serves á la carte cafeteria-style breakfast, lunch, and dinner. Located near the front desk at Yosemite Lodge. (Moderately inexpensive; open year-round)

BEER, WINE & COCKTAILS

THE AHWAHNEE BAR

The Ahwahnee Hotel's upscale bar serves draft beer, wine, cocktails, and gourmet appetizers. You can drink inside or on the outdoor patio. (Open year-round.)

THE MOUNTAIN ROOM BAR & LOUNGE

The Valley's liveliest bar, located in Yosemite Lodge. Serves beer, wine, cocktails and light appetizers. (Open year-round)

CURRY PAVILION BAR

This tiny bar, located next to the Pizza Deck, serves a handful of draft beers and cocktails. (Open spring, summer, fall)

GROCERIES

VILLAGE STORE

This large store, located in Yosemite Village, offers the best selection of groceries in the Valley—fruits, vegetables, meat, snacks, beer, wine, canned goods—and a huge selection of gifts and knickknacks. (Open year-round)

CURRY VILLAGE STORE

Located near the Curry Village parking area, this store offers a decent selection of groceries, plus firewood, ice, books, gifts, etc. (Open year-round)

OUTDOOR GEAR/SPORTING GOODS

CURRY VILLAGE MOUNTAIN SHOP

The Mountain Shop is the largest outdoor store in Yosemite, offering the best selection of hiking, camping, and rock climbing gear. Located next to the Curry Village Store. (Open year-round)

YOSEMITE VILLAGE SPORT SHOP

The Sport Shop offers a good selection of basic outdoor gear—boots, jackets, backpacking supplies, etc. Located near the Village Store. (Open year-round)

SPECIAL EVENTS

BRACEBRIDGE DINNER

Half multi-course Christmas feast, half theater-in-the-round, Bracebridge is the Ahwahnee Hotel's most famous winter tradition. First started in 1927, this Renaissance-style dinner, held several times in December, features a cast of over 100 richly costumed performers singing and dancing and serving your food. Based loosely on Washington Irving's classic account of an Old English feast, Bracebridge is exceedingly popular, exceedingly expensive, and exceedingly worth it. (www.bracebridgedinners.com, 559-253-5604)

VINTNERS' HOLIDAYS

Each November and December, the Ahwahnee Hotel hosts several multi-day wine tasting events. Packages for Vintners' Holidays include hotel reservations, wine seminars, a Meet the Vintners Reception, and a gourmet multi-course meal at the Ahwahnee Hotel. Several sessions are offered, each with a unique twist. (559-253-5635, www.yosemitepark.com)

CHEFS' HOLIDAYS

Similar to Vintners' Holidays, but with an emphasis on gourmet food. Held in January and February at the Ahwahnee Hotel. Several unique multi-day events feature cooking demonstrations, a Behind the Scenes kitchen tour, and a five-course gala dinner. (559-253-5635, www.yosemitepark.com)

YOSEMITE ASSOCIATION SEMINARS

Throughout the year the nonprofit Yosemite Association offers a wide variety of fantastic outdoor seminars focusing on such topics as geology, ecology, bird watching, painting, photography, and much more. A detailed listing of current offerings is available on their website. (www.yosemite.org)

YOSEMITE VALLEY

1 Yosemite Village   7 Bridalveil Fall   13 Curry Village

2 Yosemite Falls   8 Cathedral Beach   14 Half Dome

3 Camp 4   9 Sentinel Beach   15 Happy Isles

4 Devils Elbow   10 Sentinel Falls   16 Mirror Lake

5 El Capitan   11 Yosemite Chapel   17 Ahwahnee Hotel

6 Tunnel View   12 LeConte Memorial

Big Oak Flat Road

Northside Drive

140

Wawona Tunnel

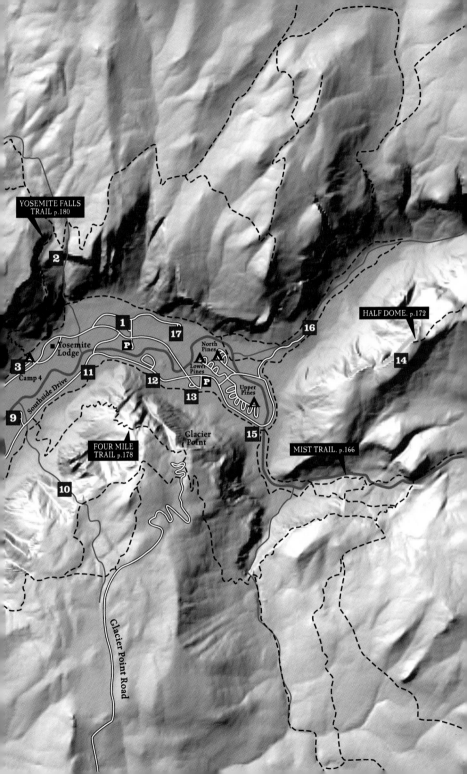

YOSEMITE FALLS
TRAIL p.180

2

HALF DOME. p.172

1

17

16

Yosemite
Lodge

North
Pines

P

14

3

Camp 4

11

Lower
Pines

P

Southside Drive

12

13

Upper
Pines

9

15

Glacier
Point

FOUR MILE
TRAIL p.178

MIST TRAIL. p.166

10

Glacier Point Road

1 Yosemite Village

This cluster of buildings is home to the official park visitor center and several shops selling gifts, books, burgers, groceries, hiking boots, camping gear—you name it. Park in front of the Village Store or use the much larger day use parking area (shuttle stop #1) just south of the main road. For shops and restaurants use shuttle stops 2, 4, & 10. For the Yosemite Visitor Center and sights listed below use shuttle stops 5 & 9.

The **Yosemite Visitor Center** should be your first stop in Yosemite Village. The front desk is staffed with knowledgeable experts ready to answer any park questions you might have, and nearby exhibits showcase Yosemite's fascinating natural history. There's also the superb Yosemite Association bookstore and an auditorium that shows the free short film *The Spirit of Yosemite* every half-hour. Adjacent to the Visitor Center is the **Yosemite Museum**, which specializes in Indian artifacts, and behind the museum is the **Yosemite Indian Village**, an outdoor replica of a traditional Ahwahneechee Indian village. Just west of the museum is the **Yosemite Cemetery**, where many early Yosemite settlers are buried. To the east of the Visitor Center is the **Ansel Adams Gallery**, filled with photographs, postcards, books, calendars, and just about anything else related to the famous photographer. The gallery also exhibits the work of up-and-coming photographers, and film and photo supplies are sold in the back. Next to the gallery is the **Yosemite Valley Wilderness Center,** the only place in the Valley where you can pick up wilderness permits required for overnight backpacks. Finally there's the **Yosemite Post Office**, which will gladly stamp Yosemite's very own zip code (95389) on your postcards and letters.

2 Yosemite Falls

This 2,425-foot, three-tiered waterfall is one of the most spectacular sights in the park. If all three tiers are taken together, Yosemite Falls is the highest waterfall in North America and the fifth-highest waterfall in the world. (Angel Falls in Venezuela is the world's highest waterfall at 3,212 feet.) Individually the three tiers form Upper Fall (1,430 feet), middle cascade (675 feet), and Lower Fall (320 feet). An easy half-mile loop heads from the shuttle stop (#6) to the base of the falls. In the spring, when the waterfall is at its peak, visitors near the base of the falls are soaked in a cool spray. The top of Yosemite Falls can be reached via the strenuous 3.8-mile Yosemite Falls Trail (p.180).

During full moon nights in April and May, a multi-colored "moonbow" often forms in Yosemite Falls. By late summer the waterfall has slowed to a trickle, but in the winter frozen spray and fallen ice form an ice cone up to 300 feet tall at the base of the upper fall.

Yosemite Falls

Black oaks in Yosemite Valley were the Ahwahneechee Indian's most important source of food, yielding several tons of acorns each fall. A multi-day feast accompanied the annual harvest, but most of the acorns were stored for winter use. Acorn flour was cooked into soup, mush, or bread.

3 Camp 4

At first glance this grungy, crowded cluster of tents seems like a campsite of last resort. But Camp 4 is one of rock climbing's holiest temples—a global mecca on a par with base camp at Mt. Everest. The story began in the 1950s, when pioneering rock climbers came to Yosemite to conquer the park's famous walls. Scraping out a meager existence in Camp 4, they spent years honing the culture and craft of modern rock climbing, pioneering techniques that would ultimately be used around the world. By day the "granite astronauts" climbed big walls; by night they discussed their exploits around roaring campfires in Camp 4. Over the years, as the popularity of rock climbing grew, Camp 4 developed a reputation as Yosemite's Climber's Camp. (Around this time a scraggly climber named Yvon Chounard began selling homemade climbing equipment in Camp 4's parking lot; Chounard later went on to found Patagonia, Inc.)

In 1997 the "Flood of the Century" washed out many of Yosemite Valley's low-lying buildings and campsites. In response, the National Park Service decided to shut down Camp 4, which lay above the floodplain, and replace it with rebuilt employee and guest housing. Upon hearing the news, a group of climbers united to save the fabled campsite. Understanding its unique role in the global history of rock climbing, they met with park service officials and pleaded their cause. Climbers from around the world flooded the park service with letters and phone calls attesting to the importance of the site. Suddenly aware of Camp 4's unique heritage, the park service agreed to keep the campsite open. In 2003 it was listed on the National Register of Historic Places.

Camp 4 has been called both "tent ghetto" and "home of the gods" by rock climbers—a fact that speaks volumes about the grungy, tribal culture of the sport. For many, Camp 4 is as much about socializing as actual climbing. It's where members of a scattered, global subculture go to meet, greet, see, and be seen. Friendships are made, gossip is swapped, rivalries are born, and life goes on pretty much as it always has since climbers made Camp 4 their unofficial home away from home.

4 Devils Elbow

Gloriously situated beneath El Capitan, this sandy bend in the Merced River is the perfect place to lounge around and watch the hours drift by. Located about 1.5 miles past Camp 4, Devils Elbow is best in the summer when the water level of the Merced has dropped. Note: sections of the riverbank are closed for the restoration of native willows and cottonwoods. Pay attention to posted signs.

Devils Elbow

5 El Capitan

This imposing granite monolith, rising 3,593 feet above the Valley floor, is arguably the most famous rock climb in the world.

During peak climbing season in the spring and fall, hundreds of world-class climbers descend on Yosemite Valley to test their mettle on El Capitan's legendary walls. On average, it takes 3–6 days to reach the top. After climbing all day, climbers spend the night on a "port-a-ledge," a collapsible platform strapped to the face of the rock, which leads to a very logical next question: How exactly does one go to the bathroom on a 3,000-foot vertical cliff? The answer (of course): very carefully. In addition to the physical, technical, and mental difficulties of the actual act, all solid human waste must be collected and carried off the cliff. For years climbers brought along homemade "poop tubes" made from sawed-off sections of PVC pipe. Today commercially available sanitary bags are the norm.

The first climber to conquer El Captain was Warren Harding, who pioneered The Nose route with two friends in 1958. Using "siege tactics" (setting fixed ropes higher and higher and rappelling down for rest and supplies), it took the team 45 days of climbing to reach the top. Royal Robbins, Harding's rival, considered such tactics poor form, and in 1960 he assembled a team that climbed The Nose in a self-contained, seven-day ascent. In 1975 Jim Bridwell led a team on the first one-day ascent of The Nose. And in 1993 female rock climber Lynn Hill became the first person to free climb The Nose. (In free climbing only body parts are used to climb; ropes and gear are used only for protection from a fall.) The following year Hill returned and free climbed The Nose in a single day. Today the current obsession is speed. In 2002 Hans Florine and Yuji Hirayama climbed The Nose in a mind-blowing 2 hours, 48 minutes, and 30 seconds!

A pullout on the road in front of El Capitan is a great place to watch climbers during the day (look for tiny black specks and their dangling gear bags). After sundown you can often see multiple climbers' lights high on the rock.

The Ahwahneechee Legend of Tutokanula

Long ago, two bear cubs wandered away from their mother and fell asleep on a rock near the Merced River. As they slept the rock rose high into the sky, and the cubs became stranded. All of the forest animals tried to climb the cliff to rescue the cubs, but no one—not fox, not coyote, not mountain lion—could reach the top. Finally a tiny inchworm called Tutoka offered his help. At first the other animals laughed, but Tutoka slowly made his way up the cliff. As the inchworm climbed, he chanted "Tu·tok ... Tu·tok ... Tu·tok·a·nu·la!" Upon reaching the top, the inchworm guided the two cubs down to safety.

El Capitan

"The modicum of moonlight that fell into this awful gorge gave to that precipice a vagueness of outline, an indefinite vastness, a ghostly and weird spirituality. Had the mountain spoken to me in audible voice ... I should hardly have been surprised."

—Horace Greeley, 1859

Climbers lights on El Capitan at night

6 Tunnel View

This stunning viewpoint is one of Yosemite's must-see destinations. Perched high above Yosemite Valley's western entrance, many of the park's most notable landmarks—Bridalveil Fall, El Capitan, Half Dome—are spread out in a picture perfect display. The sweeping panorama was immortalized by Ansel Adams in his iconic 1935 photograph *Clearing Winter Storm*, depicting the scene in the wake of a snowstorm. These days the small parking area at Tunnel View is often swarming with tourists and tour buses during the busy summer months. If you're thirsting for peace and quiet, follow the steep trail that starts in the adjacent parking area and heads to Old Inspiration Point (the original viewpoint along the old wagon road that the modern highway replaced). Follow the trail for several hundred yards and you'll be treated to equally dramatic views of Yosemite Valley high above the crowds.

Looking out over Yosemite Valley from Tunnel View, the landscape seems eternal. But the present view is far different from the one enjoyed by early tourists in the 1850s. Prior to the arrival of whites, Yosemite Valley had larger meadows and open forests with trees spaced widely apart—the result of small, regular fires set by the Ahwahneechee Indians. Mature trees survived the small fires due to thick protective bark, but unwanted vegetation—saplings encroaching upon meadows, shrubs and debris on the forest floor—were cleared out, creating open spaces that made travel and hunting much easier. Such landscapes also favored the animals that the Ahwahneechee liked to hunt. Far from being untouched, Yosemite Valley was actively modified. Then, throughout much of the 20th century, the National Park Service followed a policy of fire suppression to "preserve" Yosemite Valley, which inadvertently led to smaller meadows and overgrown forests. Today the park service sets intentional, small fires to help return Yosemite Valley to its pre-contact state. (See page 63 for more about fire in Yosemite.)

"The grandeur of the scene was softened by the haze that hung over the valley—light as gossamer—and by the clouds which partially dimmed the higher cliffs and mountains. This obscurity of vision but increased the awe with which I beheld it, and as I looked, a peculiar exalted sensation seemed to fill my whole being, and I found my eyes in tears with emotion."

—Dr. Lafayette Bunnell, 1851

Tunnel View

7 Bridalveil Fall

This elegant, 620-foot waterfall is one of Yosemite Valley's most popular sights. Frequent gusts of wind often fan out the waterfall's lower curtain, giving it the appearance of a white, lacy veil—a phenomena that inspired early explorers to name it Bridalveil. The Ahwahneechee called the waterfall *Pohono* ("Spirit of the Puffing Wind"). The headwaters of Bridalveil Creek begin near Ostrander Lake (elevation: 8,500 feet), where a small band of Indians called the Pohoneechee used to spend their summers. The Pohoneechee, like the Ahwahneechee in Yosemite Valley, were a subgroup of the Sierra Miwok Tribe.

Bridalveil Fall is most dramatic between April and June, when melting snow creates peak runoff. During this time a late afternoon rainbow can often be seen from the parking area, and a *double* rainbow can sometimes be seen near the base of the falls (reached via a quarter-mile path from the parking area).

The granite trough above Bridalveil Fall is a textbook example of a "hanging valley." Prior to the Ice Age, the Sierra Nevada Mountains were characterized by V-shaped valleys carved out by rivers over millions of years. Back then Bridalveil Creek, which forms Bridalveil Fall, flowed through a V-shaped valley that extended all the way down to the Merced River. But when Ice Age glaciers flowed through Yosemite Valley, they gouged out the junction of the Merced River and Bridalveil Creek, leaving behind a "hanging" valley. When the glaciers melted, Bridalveil Creek tumbled over the edge of the hanging valley and formed the beautiful waterfall you see today.

8 Cathedral Beach Picnic Area

This shady picnic area, nestled among ponderosa pines and incense cedars, offers great swimming in the summer along a sandy section of the Merced River. The riverbank offers tremendous views of El Capitan's southwest face, and on the opposite side of the Valley are Cathedral Spires (above), a pair of rock pinnacles rising 1,900 feet above the Valley floor. To the east of El Capitan is Three Brothers, an unusual three-tiered rock formation formed by parallel faulting, which is a fancy way of saying that the rock eroded along three major sets of diagonal cracks. In 1987 a massive rockfall sent 1.5 *million tons* of granite tumbling down from Three Brothers, leveling trees and tossing giant boulders into the Merced River hundreds of yards away. The Indian name for the humped rock formation was *Kom-po-pai-zes*, which early explorer Dr. Lafayette Bunnell recorded as "mountains playing leapfrog," This was not the actual translation, however, for Bunnell admitted that "a literal translation is not desirable." Had Bunnell been less inclined towards G-rated prose, he would have translated *Kom-po-pai-zes* as—how do I put this?—a couple engaged in an act of passion.

9 Sentinel Beach Picnic Area

This picnic area is similar to Cathedral Picnic Area, with picnic tables and a restroom nestled among a shady grove of trees. This is also the stopping point for Merced river rafters (p.31).

Three Brothers

10 Sentinel Falls

At 2,000 feet Sentinel Falls is the second-highest waterfall in Yosemite Valley (if the multiple tiers are added together). Although the waterfall dries up in the summer, towering Sentinel Rock stands guard to the left year-round. According to Josiah Whitney, 7,038-foot Sentinel Rock was named for its "fancied likeness to a gigantic watch-tower."

11 Yosemite Chapel

Graced with stunning views of Yosemite Falls, this quaint little chapel blesses dozens of marriages each year. (Call 559-253-5673 if you'd like to get hitched there.) Built in 1879, Yosemite Chapel is the oldest building in Yosemite still in use. Non-denominational services are open to the public—check the bulletin board just inside the door for current times.

12 LeConte Memorial

This tiny stone building, built in 1903, is owned by the Sierra Club and named for Dr. Joseph LeConte, a professor at U.C. Berkeley during the late 1800s and one of the co-founders of the Sierra Club. Inside you'll find exhibits about the Sierra Club and a great library filled with nature books. Open late spring to early fall. Free evening programs are offered on the weekends (check *Yosemite Today*).

Sentinel Falls

The Fire Fall

DAVID CURRY

13 Curry Village

This dense cluster of tent cabins, shower houses, shops, and snack bars throbs with activity throughout the spring, summer, and fall. Along with Yosemite Village, Curry Village is one of two main visitor hubs in Yosemite Valley.

Curry Village was first established in 1899 by David and Jennie Curry. At the time there were several hotels in the Valley, but at $2 per night "Camp Curry" undercut them by half. Its motto: "Three squares a day, a clean napkin every meal, and NO tipping!" The couple started out with seven tent cabins, but they expanded to 25 by the end of the summer. Each morning at sunrise David Curry bellowed out, "Those who do not rise for breakfast by eight am will have to postpone it until tomorrow. At eight o'clock the cook gets *hot* and burns the breakfast!"

To entertain guests after sundown, Camp Curry offered an evening program that featured music, singing, and storytelling. But the most famous attraction was the legendary Fire Fall. Every night in the summer a large fire of red fir bark was built at the edge of Glacier Point, 3,200 feet above Camp Curry. Two hours later, a call went out to "Let the Fire Fall!" The glowing coals were then pushed over the edge, and spectators were treated to a glittering cascade of falling embers. Though wildly popular, the Fire Fall was halted by the park service in 1968. The spectacle was considered out of keeping with the park's mission to preserve Yosemite Valley's natural character.

Today the original "Camp Curry" sign still hangs in Curry Village, and 427 tent cabins continue to provide Yosemite Valley's best budget lodging.

14 Half Dome

Looming over Yosemite Valley like a granite monarch, Half Dome is the park's most iconic landmark. This 8,842-foot high monolith, rising nearly 5,000 feet above the Valley floor, lures thousands of hikers to its summit each year. It can be conquered in a one-day, 12-hour push, or tackled as a two-day backpack, spending the night at Little Yosemite Valley Campground about halfway to the top. (See p.172 for hiking info.)

In 1868 the famous geologist Josiah Whitney proclaimed that Half Dome was "probably the only one of all the prominent points about the Yosemite which never has been, and never will be, trodden by human foot." Predictably, attempts to climb it were soon underway. Although practically anyone could reach the rounded backside of Half Dome, the final 975-foot, 45-degree ascent was simply too steep to hike. In 1875 Valley blacksmith George Anderson spent several weeks drilling bolts into Half Dome's backside. Standing on the bolts as he drilled new ones above, he soon reached the 13-acre summit. His rope-strung bolts remained the standard route for years, but they have since been replaced with a slightly more advanced metal cable system. In 1957 Royal Robbins led a team of rock climbers on the first ascent of Half Dome's sheer, 2,000-foot Northwest Face. The astounding five-day climb was considered the hardest route in North America at the time. Ten years later Liz Robbins, Royal's wife, became the first woman to climb the Northwest Face of Half Dome.

So what happened to the other half of Half Dome? In fact, there never was another half. When Half Dome formed millions of years ago (due to the erosion of overlying rocks), natural cracks in the dome formed a sheer northwestern face. Ice Age glaciers later knocked off additional rock, expanding the vertical face.

The Ahwahneechee Legend of Tissayak

Long ago, a woman named Tissayak and her husband Nangas traveled to Yosemite Valley from the arid plains. Exhausted after the long journey, Nangas lost his temper and hit Tissayak. As Tissayak dashed up Yosemite Valley acorns spilled out of her basket, and those acorns later grew into oak trees. When Tissayak reached Mirror Lake she drank it dry. When the thirsty Nangas approached, he grew enraged and hit her again. As Tissayak threw her basket at Nangas, the angry gods turned the couple into stone. Nangas became North Dome (with Basket Dome above) and Tissayak became Half Dome, her tears marked by dark streaks on the vertical face. For the rest of eternity the quarreling couple must now face each other in silence.

"Great is granite and Yosemite is its prophet"
—Thomas Starr King

15 Happy Isles

This leafy stretch of the Merced River, lying just east of Curry Village, is almost always buzzing with activity due to its proximity to the Mist Trail, the most popular hike in the park (p.166). The name Happy Isles comes from three nearby islands in the Merced River. The road to Happy Isles is off limits to private vehicles—visitors must walk here or take the free shuttle. A short distance from the shuttle stop is the family-friendly Nature Center at Happy Isles (open May–mid-Sept). This small museum is filled with natural history displays and serves as Yosemite's headquarters for the kid-oriented Junior Ranger Program.

16 Mirror Lake

Mirror Lake is a great destination for anyone looking to soak in natural scenery away from a crowded parking lot. The short, easy trail starts at shuttle stop #17, crosses Tenaya Creek Bridge, and then follows Tenaya Creek up to Mirror Lake. Lying in the shadow of Half Dome, the "lake" is actually a wide, calm stretch of Tenaya Creek formed by boulders that dam the water's flow. Mirror Lake is best viewed in the spring and early summer when the water level is high. For the best reflections, walk along the east side of the lake in the morning and the west side in the late afternoon. If you're looking for a longer walk, an easy four-mile loop heads up Tenaya Canyon and crosses Tenaya Creek at Snow Creek Bridge.

ROCKFALLS

On July 10, 1996, two colossal slabs of granite broke free from the cliffs 1,900 feet above Happy Isles. Roughly 70,000 tons of rock went into free fall, hitting the ground moments later at 260 mph. The granite pulverized instantly and generated a 240 mph blast of wind that uprooted trees and sent rock fragments hurtling through the air. One hiker was killed, and the Nature Center at Happy Isles barely escaped destruction. A massive dust cloud blanketed the surroundings, blackening the sky for six minutes. In the wake of the rockfall, roughly 1,000 trees lay flattened and a two-inch layer of gray dust settled over Happy Isles. The force of the impact was so powerful that it registered on seismographs over 100 miles away.

In the past 150 years over 400 rockfalls have been recorded in Yosemite Valley. Although terrifying and destructive, they are a natural part of the landscape—one of many forms of erosion that continue to shape the park. To date only 10 people have lost their lives due to rockfalls in Yosemite (out of tens of millions of visitors). The odds of encountering a rockfall in Yosemite are exceptionally slim, but you should always remain alert when walking beneath sheer cliffs.

Mirror Lake

17 Ahwahnee Hotel

The Ahwahnee is the pinnacle of luxury in Yosemite—which isn't surprising given the $400 per night price tag. (The hotel's opulent Tresider Suite, which comes with a library parlor, rents for $1,000 per night!) Still, even non-guests can enjoy a stroll through the hotel's sumptuous interior spaces or a gourmet meal in the majestic dining room (p.129). And nothing tops off a long day of hiking like a cold cocktail at the hotel's bar or outdoor patio. Guided tours of the Ahwahnee are also offered throughout the year (inquire at the concierge desk).

The Ahwahnee first opened for business in 1927. Its construction was spearheaded by Stephen Mather, the first director of the National Park Service, who wanted a world-class lodge for his favorite national park. From a distance the hotel appears to be built of stone and timber, but a closer look reveals that the "timber" is actually concrete. Several famous national park lodges had been destroyed by fire in the early 1900s, so Mather insisted that the Ahwahnee be fire resistant. To retain its rustic charm, the concrete supports were poured into wood-grain molds and painted to look like timber. Real timber was used only in the dining room.

Over the decades the Ahwahnee has played host to dozens of celebrities, including Queen Elizabeth, Eleanor Roosevelt, and John F. Kennedy (who flew into the Valley via helicopter). Lucille Ball, Desi Arnaz, and Judy Garland stayed here while filming *The Long, Long Trailer*, as did William Shatner and Leonard Nimoy while filming *Star Trek* IV. But no one can top Robert Redford's ties to the Ahwahnee: he worked here as an employee before launching his film career.

Ahwahnee dining room

The Ahwahnee's Great Lounge is famous for warm fires in the winter and tea and cookies served to guests every day at 4pm. If the room seems hauntingly familiar, there's a good reason: it was used as a model for one of the interior sets in Stanley Kubrick's 1980 film *The Shining*.

⇾᷿ THE MIST TRAIL ᷿⇽

SUMMARY The Mist Trail is the most popular trail in Yosemite—and with good reason. A relatively short hike from Yosemite Valley brings you to 317-foot Vernal Fall, where a series of stone steps climbs to the waterfall's edge. From there strong hikers can continue to the top of 594-foot Nevada Fall, which is arguably even more spectacular than Vernal Fall. Sheer cliffs, dramatic waterfalls, misty rainbows—few trails in the world deliver so much for so little effort. The downside: massive crowds throughout the summer. On busy weekends the Mist Trail often feels more like a trip to the mall than the Great Outdoors. But at least it's a mall with great scenery. Note: the Mist Trail gets its name from the drenching mist in front of Vernal Fall that soaks hikers in the spring and early summer—beware of slippery stone steps.

TRAILHEAD The Mist Trail starts in Happy Isles (shuttle stop #16) at the eastern end of Yosemite Valley. The info listed below is for a hike to the top of Nevada Fall, returning via the John Muir Trail. The moderate hike to the top of Vernal Fall is 3 miles round-trip with 1,100 feet of elevation change (2–3 hours).

TRAIL INFO

DIFFICULTY: Strenuous	**HIKING TIME:** 4–6 hours
DISTANCE: 5.8 miles, round-trip	**ELEVATION CHANGE:** 1,900 ft.

Vernal Fall

"How softly these rocks are adorned, and how fine and reassuring the company they keep, their feet among beautiful groves and meadows, their brows in the sky ... bathed in floods of water, floods of light."

—John Muir

Nevada Fall

❧ HALF DOME ☙

SUMMARY   This towering quirk of geology beckons every adventurer who sets eyes on it. It is, without question, the most fabled hike in the park. The challenging 8.5-mile trail to the top starts in Yosemite Valley, passes by Vernal and Nevada Falls, then climbs to the base of Half Dome's steep backside. From there you'll haul yourself up a pair of metal cables drilled into the rock—a vertigo-inducing experience sure to quicken any pulse. Make no mistake, this is definitely *not* a trail for the faint of heart. But if you've got the physical and mental stamina to take on Half Dome, you'll be rewarded with jaw-dropping views of Yosemite Valley and an experience you'll never forget. Strong hikers can make it round-trip in 12 hours. If you choose to hike Half Dome in two days, you must obtain wilderness permits for Little Yosemite Valley Campground, located about halfway to the top. Note: the cables are only up from late May to mid-October.

TRAILHEAD   The trail to Half Dome starts in Happy Isles (shuttle stop #16) and follows the Mist Trail (p.166) to the top of Nevada Falls. From there follow the signs to the top of Half Dome.

TRAIL INFO

DIFFICULTY: Very Strenuous   **HIKING TIME:** 12–14 hours

DISTANCE: 17 miles, round-trip   **ELEVATION CHANGE:** 4,800 ft.

Half Dome cables

View from Half Dome

⊰ FOUR MILE TRAIL ⊱

SUMMARY Millions of tourists drive to Glacier Point to check out the stunning views, but those views are even more rewarding when you've earned them via the Four Mile Trail. This is one of the best hikes in Yosemite Valley with unrivaled views of Yosemite Falls. If hiking 3,200 feet up isn't your thing, try riding the shuttle to Glacier Point (p.194) and hiking 3,200 feet *down* to Yosemite Valley. Conversely, if hiking *just* 9.2 miles isn't your thing, consider the following 11.5-mile hike: head up the Four Mile Trail, then hike 4.4 miles down the Panorama Trail to the top of Nevada Fall, then hike 2.5 miles down to Yosemite Valley via the Mist Trail (p.166). If you've got the time and the energy, this route is one of the finest in the park. (So how did the 4.6-mile Four Mile Trail get its name? The original trail, built in the 1870s by James McCauley, was four miles long.)

TRAILHEAD The Four Mile Trail starts between Sentinel Beach and Swinging Bridge on Southside Drive.

TRAIL INFO

DIFFICULTY: Strenuous

HIKING TIME: 5–7 hours

DISTANCE: 9.2 miles, round-trip

ELEVATION CHANGE: 3,200 ft.

Happy Isles

Curry Village

Glacier Point

Washburn Point

Sentinel Dome

Union Point

Chapel

Southside Drive

Merced River

Sentinel Rock

Sentinel Fall

Four Mile Trail

Swinging Bridge

Northside Drive

Sentinel Beach

～ YOSEMITE FALLS ～

SUMMARY If you love 2,400 foot waterfalls and strenuous hikes, it doesn't get better than this. You'll pant and sweat all the way to the top, but there's no better way to revel in the majesty of Yosemite Falls. Along the way you'll be treated to sweeping views of Yosemite Valley and amazing glimpses of Upper Yosemite Fall. The top of the trail follows a notch in the cliff that brings you above the waterfall, and from there a narrow path drops down to a fenced-in ledge beside the lip of Upper Yosemite Fall. If you're afraid of heights, the fenced-in ledge is probably not for you. But for those who revel in dramatic views, it's well worth the effort. If you don't feel like climbing all the way to the top, Columbia Point (1.2 miles from the trailhead) makes a good destination with sweeping views of the Valley.

TRAILHEAD The trail to the top of Yosemite Falls starts at Camp 4. Take the shuttle to Yosemite Lodge (stop #7), and cross the street to Camp 4. The hike starts between the parking area and the campground.

TRAIL INFO

DIFFICULTY: Strenuous   **HIKING TIME:** 4–5 hours

DISTANCE: 7.6 miles, round-trip   **ELEVATION CHANGE:** 2,600 ft.

Upper
Yosemite Fall

Middle
Yosemite Fall

Lower
Yosemite Fall

Columbia
Rock

Eagle
Peak

Three Brothers

Yosemite
Lodge

Camp 4

Northside Drive

Southside Drive

Leidig
Meadow

View from Columbia Point

"It is in no scene or scenes the chasm consists, but in the miles of scenery where cliffs of awful height and rocks of vast magnitude and of varied and exquisite coloring, are banked and fringed and draped and shadowed by the tender foliage of noble and lovely trees ... associated with the most tranquil meadows, the most playful streams, and every variety of soft and peaceful pastoral beauty."

—Frederick Law Olmstead

"Here the view is perfectly free down into the heart of the bright irised throng of comet-like streamers into which the whole ponderous volume of the fall separates, two or three hundred feet below the brow. So glorious a display of pure wildness, acting at close range while cut off from all the world beside, is terribly impressive."

—John Muir

Top of Yosemite Falls

GLACIER POINT ROAD

★ ★ ★ ★ ★

Introduction 189
Map 190
Sights 191
Hiking 198

GLACIER POINT ROAD

THIS 16-MILE ROAD wraps around Yosemite Valley's south rim on its way to Glacier Point, one of the most stunning and accessible viewpoints in the park. Perched 3,200 feet above the Valley floor, you'll be treated to jaw-dropping views of Half Dome and a panorama of Sierra spectacles: Yosemite Falls, North Dome, Clouds Rest, Tenaya Canyon, the Royal Arches. Meanwhile nearby Washburn Point offers equally dramatic views of Nevada Fall, Vernal Fall, and the Clark Range. Even if you're only in Yosemite for a day, no first time visitor should leave the park without a visit to Glacier Point.

Most people drive to Glacier Point, revel in the scenery, then turn around and drive back. There's nothing wrong with that, but if you've got the time Glacier Point Road also has some terrific day hikes. A handful of trails venture along Yosemite Valley's south rim to sweeping viewpoints—all of which are mercifully less crowded than any viewpoint accessible by car—and free ranger-led hikes are often offered (check *Yosemite Today* for seasonal dates and times). If you'd like to spend a day or two exploring the trails along Glacier Point Road, spend the night at Bridalveil Creek Campground (p.38).

Glacier Point is roughly 30 driving miles from Yosemite Valley—about an hour one-way. As you drive along Glacier Point Road, you'll notice a handful of roadside meadows. Due to their high elevations, these meadows are often flower-filled long after the wildflowers have withered in Yosemite Valley.

If you don't feel like driving, you can purchase a ticket for the four-hour Glacier Point Tour ($30 adult, $20 child, 209-372-1240), which leaves Yosemite Valley twice daily from June to October. You can also ride the bus one-way to Glacier Point, then hike down the Four Mile Trail (p.178) or the Panorama Trail, which heads to Nevada Fall and the Mist Trail (p.166).

In the winter and early spring most of Glacier Point Road is closed due to heavy snow, but the first six miles are plowed to Badger Pass Ski Area, a small resort with a handful of lifts. Free winter shuttles run between Yosemite Valley hotels and Badger Pass, and free ranger-led snowshoe walks are offered daily (check *Yosemite Today*). Cross country skiers can explore dozens of miles of nearby trails or plan an overnight trip to Glacier Point or Ostrander Lake, both of which offer overnight accommodations (p.30). Note: four-wheel drive or tire chains are required for all vehicles heading to Badger Pass in the winter.

Left: Half Dome from Glacier Point

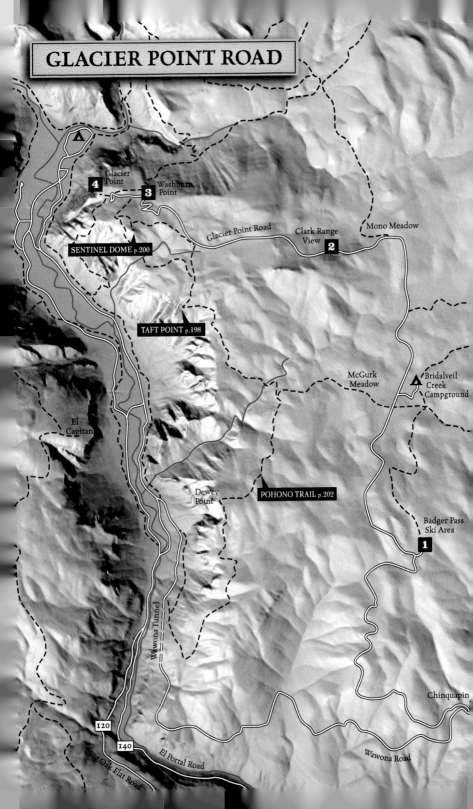

GLACIER POINT ROAD

4 Glacier Point

3 Washburn Point

Glacier Point Road

2 Clark Range View

Mono Meadow

SENTINEL DOME p.200

TAFT POINT p.198

McGurk Meadow

Bridalveil Creek Campground

El Capitan

Dewey Point

POHONO TRAIL p.202

Badger Pass Ski Area

1

Wawona Tunnel

Chinquapin

I20

I40

El Portal Road

Big Oak Flat Road

Wawona Road

1 Badger Pass Ski Area

Badger Pass—the oldest ski resort in California—offers five lifts and ten runs for skiers and snowboarders. There's not much challenging terrain, but the short lift lines and relatively cheap tickets make Badger Pass a great family and beginner slope. Cross country skiers will love the 90 miles of marked trails and 25 miles of machine-groomed track. Ski season generally runs mid-December to late March, depending on conditions. Equipment rentals and ski instruction are available, and a small base lodge serves food and drinks. Weekend tickets cost about $40 for adults, $15 for kids. Discounts mid-week. (209-372-8430, www.badgerpass.com)

2 Clark Range View

This small pullout showcases great views of the Clark Range, one of the most rugged and remote mountain ranges in the park. In the foreground is Mt. Starr King, a uniquely shaped 9,092-foot granite dome named for Thomas Starr King, a famous Unitarian minister who visited Yosemite Valley in the 1860s and helped promote the park. Beyond Mt. Starr King is 11,522-foot Mt. Clark, the highest peak in the Clark Range. Both the peak and the range were named after Galen Clark, the first Guardian of Yosemite (p.102).

3 Washburn Point

This large turnout features a stunning view framed by Half Dome on the left and conical Mt. Starr King on the right. In the center is Merced Canyon, home to two of the park's most impressive waterfalls: Nevada Fall (594 feet) and Vernal Fall (317 feet). When the Merced River is swollen with snowmelt in the spring, the roar of these waterfalls echoes all the way to Washburn Point.

Moments before the Merced River tumbles down Nevada Fall, the water is churned and frothed by a series of violent rapids, giving the waterfall an exceptional white color that inspired early explorers to name it Nevada (Spanish for "Snow"). Vernal Fall, below, was named for its "cool, vernal spray." Both waterfalls can be viewed up close along the popular Mist Trail (p.166).

The unique view from Washburn Point reveals that Half Dome isn't really half of a dome. Over 70% of the dome remains intact. And despite its rounded profile, Half Dome was never covered by glaciers. Its unique shape formed over millions of years due to the exfoliation of overlying rock layers. Although a massive Ice Age glacier once filled Yosemite Valley to the brim, Half Dome's summit always remained at least 800 feet above the ice. During this time Liberty Cap—the rounded rock formation just left of Nevada Falls—was buried under several hundred feet of ice.

"It [Half Dome] strikes even the most casual observer as a new revelation in mountain forms; its existence would be considered an impossibility if it were not there before us in all its reality; it is a unique thing in mountain scenery, and nothing even approaching it can be found except in the Sierra Nevada."

Washburn Point

4 Glacier Point

The views from 7,214-foot Glacier Point are among the most spectacular in Yosemite—and, for that matter, in all of California. Many of Yosemite Valley's most famous features—Half Dome, Yosemite Falls, Royal Arches, North Dome—can be seen in a single, sweeping panorama. Glacier Point is reached via a short, paved path from the large parking area. Along the way you'll pass the chalet-style Glacier Point Snack Shop and the small Geology Hut, which features diagrams detailing the geologic processes that helped shape Yosemite Valley. Just below the Geology Hut is a pair of free binoculars (great for checking out ant-like hikers on top of Half Dome) and a metal plaque that points out famous landmarks and distant peaks. Glacier Point itself is a small platform surrounded by a protective railing. Peak over the edge and you'll stare 3,214 feet straight down to the floor of Yosemite Valley. At night, Glacier Point offers exceptional views of the night sky, and every Friday and Saturday in the summer telescopes are set up for the hour-long "Stars Over Yosemite" program. Free sunset ranger talks are also offered.

Glacier Point Hotel, 1916

For years Glacier Point was only accessible via the 4-mile trail from Yosemite Valley. The trail was the brainchild of James McCauley, who financed its construction in 1871 and charged a toll of $1 per hiker. In 1878 McCauley opened The Mountain House Hotel at Glacier Point, which was later joined by the Glacier Point Hotel in 1917. Both structures burned down in 1969 and were never rebuilt.

Waking up every day on the rim of Yosemite Valley, McCauley soon gave in to the most basic of human impulses and started throwing things off of it. Legend has it that he would bring his guests to Glacier Point, then shock them by tossing a live hen over the edge. As the poor bird plummeted through the air McCauley laughed, assuring the horrified onlookers that the hen would survive. The guests were often shocked when, walking down the Four Mile Trail, they encountered the weary hen slowly pecking its way back to Glacier Point.

"Nature chose for tool not the earthquake or lightening to rent and split asunder, not the stormy torrent or eroding rain, but the tender snow-flowers noiselessly falling through unnumbered centuries ..."

—John Muir

⊸ TAFT POINT ⊱

SUMMARY   This easy hike—more like a casual stroll—wanders through a shady forest before depositing you at Taft Point: a vertigo-inducing precipice that looms over Yosemite Valley. A small metal railing is all that protects you from the stomach-churning, 3,500-foot drop. Taft Point (7,503 feet) offers great views of Yosemite Falls and the Merced River twisting along the Valley Floor, but the sensational views of El Capitan are what really sets this spot apart. Nearby are the famous Taft Point Fissures, which plummet hundreds of feet straight down, these dramatic cracks formed over tens of thousands of years as erosion chipped away at natural cracks in the bedrock. One of the fissures has a rock lodged in it. Taft Point was named for President William Taft, who visited Yosemite in 1909.

TRAILHEAD   The Taft Point trail starts from Taft Point/Sentinel Dome parking area (14 miles east of Chinquapin; 7 miles west of Glacier Point). The parking area is easily noticed by its open setting and small restroom.

TRAIL INFO

RATING: Easy

HIKING TIME: 1 hour

DISTANCE: 2.2 miles, round-trip

ELEVATION CHANGE: 250 feet

Pohono Trail

Taft Point

Northside Drive

Merced River

Southside Drive

Sentinel Falls

Sentinel Rock

Sentinel Dome

Four Mile Trail

Washburn Point

Glacier Point

❧ SENTINEL DOME ❧

SUMMARY This short hike offers plenty of bang for your buck, with 360-degree views from the top of 8,122-foot Sentinel Dome (the second highest point on Yosemite Valley's rim after Half Dome). Perched 1,000 feet higher than Glacier Point, Sentinel Dome offers sweeping views of Yosemite Valley's north rim and unrivaled panoramas of the surrounding High Sierra peaks—identified by a metal plaque embedded in a boulder at the summit. Nearby is the fallen skeleton of a gnarled Jeffrey pine. This wind-contorted tree, made famous by Ansel Adams, was over 400 years old when it died during a drought in the mid-1970s. Remarkably, the skeleton remained standing until 2003. Sentinel Dome makes a fantastic sunset destination for anyone looking to escape the crowds at Glacier Point. As Dr. Joseph LeConte put it after witnessing a sunset from Sentinel Dome in 1870: "Such a sunset, combined with such a view, I never imagined."

TRAILHEAD The Sentinel Dome trail starts from Taft Point/Sentinel Dome parking area (14 miles east of Chinquapin; 7 miles west of Glacier Point). The parking area is easily noticed by its open setting and small restroom.

◄ **TRAIL INFO** ►

RATING: Easy

HIKING TIME: 1 hour

DISTANCE: 2.2 miles, round-trip

ELEVATION CHANGE: 380 feet

Pohono Trail

Northside Drive

Merced River

Southside Drive

Taft Point

Sentinel Falls

Sentinel Rock

Sentinel Dome

P

Four Mile Trail

P

Washburn Point

P

Glacier Point

⚜ POHONO TRAIL ⚜

SUMMARY On busy weekends when Yosemite Valley is a crowded, congested mess, the Pohono trail offers hikers a well-earned sense of solitude. Despite its breathtaking views of Bridalveil Fall, Ribbon Fall, and El Capitan, the Pohono trail remains relatively uncrowded. While other tourists are trying to find a parking space, you can soak in the Valley's majesty high above it all. Whether you're day hiking or backpacking, the Pohono Trail never disappoints. Although the complete 13.8-mile Pohono Trail stretches from Tunnel View (p.146) to Taft Point (p.198), you can reach the most spectacular viewpoints—Dewey Point, Crocker Point (above), Stanford Point—via a short hike from Glacier Point Road. The hiking distance listed below is for a round-trip hike from the McGurk Meadow trailhead to Dewey Point.

TRAILHEAD The McGurk Meadow trailhead is located 7.5 miles from the start of Glacier Point Road on the left. (Park in the pullout 100 yards up the road.) Follow the trail 1.9 miles to the junction of the Pohono Trail and turn left towards Dewey Point. Note: overnight camping is not allowed to the right of the junction.

◀ TRAIL INFO ▶

RATING: Moderate

HIKING TIME: 4 hours

DISTANCE: 7.8 miles, round-trip

ELEVATION CHANGE: 300 feet

Dewey Point

⊲ THE CLARK RANGE ⟿

SUMMARY For serious backpackers who aren't afraid of multiple days in the wilderness and several thousand feet of elevation change, few hikes in the park are as rewarding as the Clark Range. Seldom visited due to its rugged terrain, the range features pristine alpine lakes, rocky above-treeline landscapes, and the highest pass in the park: Red Peak Pass (11,200 feet). Highlights near the trail include Ottoway Lakes, Red Peak Pass, and gorgeous Red Devil Lake, where enchanting granite shores offer stunning views of the Clark Range during the day and wide open star gazing at night. To finish off the trip in style, reserve a tent cabin at Merced High Sierra Camp and treat yourself to a bed, a hot shower, and a home-cooked meal on your last night. Finish the hike by heading down the Mist Trail to Happy Isles in Yosemite Valley.

TRAILHEAD The hike starts at the Mono Meadows trailhead off Glacier Point Road. Unless you have two cars to shuttle between the start and the finish, leave your car in Yosemite Valley and ride the Glacier Point shuttle to the Mono Meadows trailhead.

TRAIL INFO

RATING: Very Strenuous

HIKING TIME: 6–7 days

DISTANCE: 46.5 miles

ELEVATION CHANGE: 7,000 ft.

THE CLARK RANGE

Mt.
Florence

Ansel
Adams
Wilderness

Isberg
Pass

Washburn
Lake

Red Devil
Lake

Edna
Lake

Red
Peak
Pass

Merced Lake
High Sierra Camp

Merced
Lake

The Clark Range

Red
Peak

Ottoway
Lakes

Gray
Peak

Mt.
Clark

Lower
Merced
Pass Lake

Clouds
Rest

Little
Yosemite
Valley

Mt. Starr
King

Half
Dome

Ostrander
Lake

Glacier
Point

Yosemite Valley

Mono
Meadow

Glacier Point Road

Hiking below Red Peak Pass

Red Devil Lake

TIOGA ROAD

⭐ ⭐ ⭐ ⭐ ⭐

Introduction 215
Map 216
Sights 218
Hiking 224

TIOGA ROAD

THIS 46-MILE ROAD twists deep into the heart of Yosemite, climbing 3,750 feet to the Sierra's crest and showcasing some of the park's finest alpine scenery. After you've gotten your fill of Yosemite Valley and Glacier Point, Tioga Road should be next on your list. Highlights include Olmstead Point, an open panorama with bold views of Clouds Rest and Half Dome, and Tenaya Lake, where icy waters reflect massive granite domes towering above its shore. Past Tenaya Lake Tioga Road skirts Tuolumne Meadows (p.241), then climbs to Tioga Pass—at 9,941 feet, the highest paved road in California. The road then exits the park and plunges over 3,000 feet to the eastern deserts at the base of the Sierra Nevada.

In winter Tioga Road is closed due to heavy snow. When the first snowfall hits (generally by mid-November) Tioga Road shuts down. Its reopening date in the spring depends entirely upon winter snowfall. In 1998 the road was closed until July 1 (a record), but generally Tioga Road opens around mid-May.

Tioga Road begins its ascent at Crane Flat, 16 miles northwest of Yosemite Valley along Big Oak Flat Road (Highway 120). There's a gas station and minimart at Crane Flat. If your tank is running low, it's a good idea to fill up here. The next gas station is located in Tuolumne Meadows, 39 miles distant.

Head northwest from Crane Flat along Tioga Road and soon you'll reach the Tuolumne Grove of giant sequoias. (Another grove of giant sequoias, the Merced Grove, is located 3.5 miles northeast of Crane along Big Oak Flat Road; the Merced Grove showcases about 20 large trees, reached via a 2-mile path.) Past the Tuolumne Grove, Tioga Road ascends through a long stretch of forest, passing turnoffs for White Wolf Lodge and several campgrounds. Eventually the forest gives way to open views, which become increasingly stunning as you climb higher and higher.

Along the way to Tuolumne Meadows, Tioga Road offers access to some of the finest hikes and backpacks in the park, including Clouds Rest, 10 Lakes, and two popular High Sierra Camps (May Lake and Sunrise), and a descent to North Dome, which overlooks Yosemite Valley. Although often ignored by first time visitors, these hikes are among the finest in the park.

Throughout the summer a free shuttle runs between Olmstead Point and Tioga Pass (check *Yosemite Today* for seasonal times and dates). There's also the Tuolumne Meadows Tour & Hikers Bus, which makes a daily run between Yosemite Valley and Tuolumne Meadows, stopping at popular Tioga Road viewpoints and trailheads along the way (209-372-1240).

Left: Clouds Rest from Olmstead Point

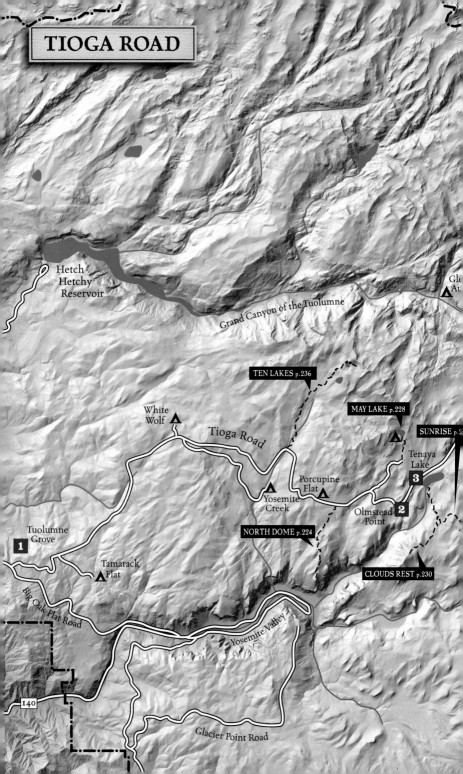

TIOGA ROAD

Hetch
Hetchy
Reservoir

Grand Canyon of the Tuolumne

Gl
Au

TEN LAKES p.236

White
Wolf

Tioga Road

MAY LAKE p.228

SUNRISE p.2

Tenaya
Lake

Porcupine
Flat

Yosemite
Creek

3

Olmstead
Point

2

NORTH DOME p.224

Tuolumne
Grove

1

Tamarack
Flat

CLOUDS REST p.230

Big Oak Flat Road

Yosemite Valley

140

Glacier Point Road

Mono Lake

Lee
Vining

120

Tioga
Pass

Tuolumne
Meadows

395

1 Tuolumne Grove

This small grove of giant sequoias is often overshadowed by the more famous Mariposa Grove in Wawona, but the Tuolumne Grove is definitely worth a visit if you're enchanted by the big trees. The grove is located about a half mile past the Crane Flat junction. A two-mile round trip path starts from the parking area and drops about 500 feet as it passes by 25 giant sequoias. Among the notables: a tree with a tunnel cut through the trunk (the tunnel was cut in 1878), and a giant tree that rises nearly 300 feet—one of the tallest giant sequoias in the world. (For more on giant sequoias, see p.68)

2 Olmstead Point

Olmstead Point offers the most dramatic view along Tioga Road, including an unusual look at Half Dome's backside. Even more impressive is the striking profile of Clouds Rest, a billowing 9,926-foot granite mountain that rises 4,500 feet above Tenaya Canyon. During the Ice Age a massive glacier filled Tenaya Canyon as it flowed towards Yosemite Valley. Olmstead Point was also buried under the ice, and the bedrock here was smoothed and polished by the glacier as it passed over the rocks. When the glacier melted, boulders embedded in the ice settled on the bedrock. These boulders, called glacial erratics, are still there today. Several fine examples of glacial erratics can be seen along the quarter-mile geology trail that starts at Olmstead Point.

Half Dome from Olmstead Point

Clouds Rest & Half Dome from Olmstead Point

"Clouds Rest was fairly enveloped in drifting gossamer films, and the Half Dome loomed up in the garish light like a majestic, living creature clad in the same gauzy, wind-woven drapery."

—John Muir

3 Tenaya Lake

Lying at an elevation of 8,149 feet, this stunning alpine lake is a great place to take a break and bask in the glorious scenery. Several picnic areas are located alongside the road, and an easy two-mile trail skirts the lake's southeastern shore. You can pick up the trail from the sandy beach at the northeastern end of the lake. The natural beach, a popular destination on hot summer days, is the result of freeze-thaw cycles in the winter. When the lake freezes, cracks form in the ice that often fill with water on warm days. When temperatures once again drop below freezing, the water in the cracks freezes and expands, pushing the previously formed ice out towards the shore. As the ice pushes outward, sediment on the bottom of the lake is pushed towards the shore, forming the sandy beach.

Tenaya Lake, like many lakes in the Sierra Nevada, formed when a massive glacier scooped out a basin in the bedrock. In the depths of the Ice Age, the ice here was over 2,000 feet deep. When the glacier melted, the basin filled with water and formed a lake. Today the southwest end of 180-foot deep Tenaya Lake is still partially dammed by debris left in the glacier's wake.

The Ahwahneechee Indians called Tenaya Lake *Pywiack*, "Lake of Shining Rocks." The name Tenaya was given by the Mariposa Battalion, a local militia organized by whites to remove Indians from the mountains. On May 22, 1851 the Battalion captured several dozen Ahwahneechee hiding near the shores of Pywiack. After marching the Indians out of the mountains, Battalion members named the lake Tenaya after the chief of the Ahwahneechee tribe.

Our camp at Lake Tenaya was especially memorable. After supper and some talk by the fire, LeConte and I sauntered through the pine groves to the shore and sat down on a big rock that stands out a little way in the water. The full moon and the stars filled the lake with light ... a slight breeze ruffled the surface, giving rise to ever-changing pictures of wondrous brightness. At first we talked freely, admiring the silvery masses and ripples of light, and the mystic, wavering dance of the stars and rocks and shadows reflected in the unstable mirror. But soon came perfect stillness, earth and sky were inseparably blended and spiritualized, and we could only gaze on the celestial vision in devout, silent, wondering admiration.

—John Muir

❧ NORTH DOME ☙

SUMMARY   Most hikes to the rim of Yosemite Valley start in the Valley and require several thousand feet of hiking up. But North Dome is reached via a one-way 4.5-mile trail that heads 600 feet *down* from Tioga Road. You'll still have to hike 600 feet up on the return (with a few extra ups and downs thrown in for good measure), but the effort is worth it. Perched high on top of 7,542-foot North Dome, you'll be treated to sweeping views of Yosemite Valley. To your left, Half Dome's terrifyingly sheer 2,000-foot northwest face looms above. Although normally done as a day hike, North Dome also makes a great backpack. The forested recess behind North Dome has several great campsites, and sunsets here are among the most spectacular in the park. Backpacking note: there is no water near North Dome—so plan on filling up at one of the several streams you'll encounter early on in the hike.

TRAILHEAD   North Dome's trailhead is located at Porcupine Creek (25 miles east of Crane Flat; 15 miles west of Tuolumne Meadows).

TRAIL INFO

RATING: Moderate

HIKING TIME: 4–5 hours

DISTANCE: 9 miles, round-trip

ELEVATION CHANGE: 600 feet

NORTH DOME

Coyote
Rocks

Porcupine
Flat

Mt.
Watkins

Indian
Rock

Watkins
Pinnacles

Basket
Dome

Snow
Creek
Falls

Tenaya Canyon

North
Dome

Washington
Column

Mirror
Lake

Half Dome

Lost Lake

Norrth Dome is one of many granite domes in Yosemite that formed when the bedrock eroded along concentric cracks, flaking off like layers of an onion. But why are the domes still bare when the surrounding scenery is covered in forest? A phenomenon called *ice creep* is party responsible for the absence of vegetation. When snow accumulates in the winter, the bottom layers of snow compress into ice. As sunlight warms the snow, water seeps under the ice and lubricates the rock. The snowpack then slides down the granite and scrapes away accumulated soil and vegetation. Although a few cracks in the granite retain enough soil for some plants to grow, most of the dome remains bare.

⊸ MAY LAKE H.S.C. ᔕ

SUMMARY   May Lake is famous as Yosemite's most accessible High Sierra Camp. The trail to May Lake is just 1.2 miles long with only 500 feet of elevation change. But even if you haven't reserved a night in one of the comfy tent cabins, this beautiful alpine lake (elevation: 9,350 feet) still makes a great day hike or overnight backpack. Looming above the lake is 10,850-foot Mount Hoffman, the geographic center of the park. Although there's no official trail to the top, Mt. Hoffman's summit is a popular destination reached via a 2-mile *un*official trail. If you're comfortable hiking off trail and feel like you can handle the strenuous ascent, Mount Hoffman is a superb destination with sweeping 360-degree views. As John Muir put it when describing how best to spend one's time in Yosemite: "Go straight to Mt. Hoffman ... From the summit nearly all the Yosemite park is displayed like a map."

TRAILHEAD   Turn onto May Lake Road (27 miles east of Crane Flat; 20 miles west of Tuolumne Meadows) and follow the road two miles to the trailhead.

◆ TRAIL INFO ◆

RATING: Easy	**HIKING TIME:** 2 hours
DISTANCE: 2.4 miles, round-trip	**ELEVATION CHANGE:** 500 feet

Mt. Hoffman

May Lake

May Lake
High Sierra Camp

Snow Creek

Snow
Flat

May Lake Road

Tioga Road

Tioga Road

Olmstead
Point

❧ CLOUDS REST ❧

SUMMARY Thousands of ambitious hikers set their sights on Half Dome, but savvy Yosemite connoisseurs know that 9,926-foot Clouds Rest offers better views in a shorter distance with mercifully fewer crowds. Nothing against Half Dome—it still offers fantastic views of Yosemite Valley. But Clouds Rest offers great views of the Valley, plus amazing views of the High Sierra, *plus* incredible views 1,000 feet above Half Dome! Simply put: Clouds Rest should be in any serious Yosemite hiker's top five. The trail starts near Tenaya Lake and soon encounters a steep, thousand-foot, switchback-laden ascent. This is toughest part of the hike (and it sure is nice to get it out of the way at the start). Although Clouds Rest is easily done in a day, there are several good campsites along the way for backpackers.

TRAILHEAD The trail to Clouds Rest starts at the Sunrise Lakes Trailhead at the southwest end of Tenaya Lake. After reaching the top of the steep ascent, the trail splits. Follow the signs to Clouds Rest.

TRAIL INFO

RATING: Strenuous

DISTANCE: 14.4 miles, round-trip

HIKING TIME: 7–8 hours

ELEVATION CHANGE: 2,200 ft.

View from Clouds Rest

∼ SUNRISE H.S.C. ∽

SUMMARY The lush meadow at Sunrise High Sierra Camp offers weary hikers the ultimate in alpine relaxation. Often waterlogged and spongy in the early summer, by mid-summer it's a wildflower-strewn paradise with a serpentine creek flowing through the center. Sparkling views of the surrounding granite peaks leave no doubt why Sunrise was included on the John Muir Trail. But even without the lure of the High Sierra Camp, Sunrise Meadow would still be a popular backpacking destination. Several exceptional campsites are perched on a rise overlooking the meadow, and campers are treated to (drum roll, please!) composting toilets.

TRAILHEAD The most direct route to Sunrise High Sierra Camp (info listed below) starts at the Sunrise Lakes Trailhead at the southwest end of Tenaya Lake. An alternate route starts in Tuolumne Meadows at the Cathedral Lakes Trailhead (p.250) and follows the John Muir Trail down to Sunrise Meadow. Although easier, the Cathedral Lake route is slightly longer (13.2 miles round-trip, 1,300 feet elevation change).

TRAIL INFO

RATING: Strenuous

HIKING TIME: 6–7 hours

DISTANCE: 10.4 miles, round-trip

ELEVATION CHANGE: 1,600 ft.

⌐ TEN LAKES ⌐

SUMMARY This secluded cluster of lakes is nestled in a granite basin at about 9,000 feet. Despite the name, there are only seven lakes at Ten Lakes (three previously counted bodies of water are now considered ponds). Numerical shortfall aside, Ten Lakes makes a good, long day hike and a superb overnight backpack. There's great fishing, and because the lakes lie below 9,600 feet campfires are allowed at night. The trail to Ten Lakes climbs gradually to Half Moon Meadow, then makes a steep ascent to 9,500-foot Ten Lakes Pass, where you'll be treated to sweeping views of the High Sierra, including Mt. Conness and the Sawtooth Ridge. From Ten Lakes Pass descend 500 feet into Ten Lakes Basin. A few hundred yards north of the lakes, the outer rim of Ten Lakes Basin drops thousands of feet into the Grand Canyon of the Tuolumne River (p.276).

TRAILHEAD The hike starts at the Ten Lakes trailhead (20 miles east of crane flat; 26 miles west of Tuolumne Meadows). There's a good-sized parking lot across the road from the trailhead.

TRAIL INFO

RATING: Strenuous   **HIKING TIME:** 6–7 hours
DISTANCE: 12.8 miles, round-trip   **ELEVATION CHANGE:** 2,000 ft.

Grand Canyon of the Tuolumne

Colby Mtn.

Ten Lakes Pass

Ten Lakes

Halfmoon Meadow

Grant Lakes

P

Tioga Road

Mt. Hoffman

May Lake

May Lake High Sierra Camp

May Lake Rd.

TUOLUMNE MEADOWS

★ ★ ★ ★ ★

Introduction 241
Basics 242
Map 244
Sights 245
Hiking 248

TUOLUMNE MEADOWS

LYING AT 8,600 feet, Tuolumne Meadows is the gateway to Yosemite's High Sierra—a stunning wilderness of flowery meadows, snow-capped peaks, and oceans of sparkling granite. Hiking trails radiate out from Tuolumne Meadows in all directions, offering hikers and rock climbers access to Yosemite's alpine wonderland. Whether you're looking for an easy stroll, a moderate day hike, or a strenuous week-long backpack, Tuolumne Meadows has it all. As the Sierra Nevada's largest subalpine meadow, it's also a great place to just kick back and relax.

In the winter Tuolumne Meadows is often buried under 10–12 feet of snow. When the snow melts, High Sierra enthusiasts flee the lowlands for Tuolumne's mountain charms. For thousands of years the Ahwahneechee Indians journeyed from Yosemite Valley to Tuolumne Meadows to trade with the Mono Indians and escape the Valley's summer heat. Fast forward to the present—not much has changed. In July and August, when Yosemite Valley is plagued with heat spells and tourist hordes, savvy Yosemite visitors head to Tuolumne to cool off high above it all. Temperatures in Tuolumne Meadows are generally 15 to 20 degrees cooler than in Yosemite Valley. And while not entirely uncrowded, Tuolumne Meadows never feels like a carnival. Besides, true Sierra solitude is never more than a hike away.

When it comes to Tuolumne hiking, timing is everything. Arrive too soon and many trails will still be covered in snow. Arrive just after the snow melts and you'll be fighting off swarms of mosquitoes. Arrive after the mosquitoes die down and you'll be treated to breathtaking Sierra splendor. Check the park's official website (www.nps.gov/yose) for current trail conditions and ask about mosquitoes before hitting the trail. August and September are consistently good months for hiking in Tuolumne, but September usually brings the first frost. By late September Tuolumne nights are often downright cold.

No matter when you visit Tuolumne, plan on bringing warm clothes. Summer days are famously sunny and warm, but nights can get chilly. Afternoon thundershowers, though infrequent, are entirely possible, and summer snow flurries, though *very* rare, can occur at any time.

Sweaty hiker note: hot showers can be purchased at Tuolumne Lodge by non-guests in the afternoon.

Tuolumne Meadows
BASICS

GETTING TO TUOLUMNE MEADOWS

Tuolumne meadows is located along Tioga Road—55 miles from Yosemite Valley and 13 miles from the town of Lee Vining at the eastern base of the Sierra. Throughout the summer the Tuolumne Meadows Tour & Hikers Bus makes a daily run between Yosemite Valley and Tuolumne Meadows (209-372-1240).

GETTING AROUND TUOLUMNE

Throughout the summer a free shuttle runs between Olmstead Point and Tioga Pass (check *Yosemite Today* for seasonal hours and dates).

LODGING & CAMPING

See Tuolumne Lodge and Tuolumne Campground (p.37).

SERVICES

TUOLUMNE MEADOWS VISITOR CENTER
This small visitor center is a great place to get up-to-date Tuolumne info: trail conditions, shuttle schedules, weather reports, etc. There are also natural history exhibits and a small bookstore. Open through late September. (209-372-0263)

WILDERNESS CENTER
Pick up wilderness permits at this small building, located a half mile east of Tuolumne Campground just off Tioga Road. (209-372-8427)

TUOLUMNE STORE
This seasonal store sells groceries, beer, wine, books, and basic camping supplies. Located just west of Tuolumne Campground. (209-372-8428)

TUOLUMNE MOUNTAIN SHOP
This small store sells an ample selection of outdoor gear—everything from tents to climbing shoes. Located just west of the Tuolumne Store on Tioga Road.

GAS
Located next to the Sport Shop. Accepts 24-hour credit card payment.

ACTIVITIES

RANGER PROGRAMS
Free ranger-led walks, hikes, and campfire programs are offered throughout the summer and into the fall (check *Yosemite Today* for seasonal dates and times).

YOSEMITE MOUNTAINEERING SCHOOL
Like its counterpart in Yosemite Valley, the Yosemite Mountaineering School in Tuolumne offers rock climbing lessons for all abilities. (209-372-8435)

TUOLUMNE MEADOWS STABLES
The Tuolumne Meadows Stables offers horseback rides along several nearby trails. Options include 2-hour rides, 4-hour rides, half-day rides, full-day rides, and multi-day pack trips. (209-372-8427)

DINING

TUOLUMNE GRILL
Cheap burgers, salads, and sandwiches. It's hardly gourmet, but it can definitely hit the spot. Located next to the Tuolumne Store (Inexpensive, Brk-Lnch-Din)

TUOLUMNE LODGE
Tuolumne Lodge offers the only sit down dining experience in Tuolumne Meadows. Great food is served to friendly diners seated in random groups at large tables. Reservations are required for dinner. Located next to the front office at Tuolumne Lodge. (Moderately priced, Breakfast & Dinner, 209-372-8413)

TIOGA PASS RESORT
More than a wayside restaurant, this place is a High Sierra institution. Fans return again and again for the great food and cozy atmosphere. The food is high on quality, low on pretension, and full of 9,000-foot alpine charm. Located two miles east of Tioga Pass. (Moderately priced, Brk-Lnch-Din, 209-372-4471)

MOBILE GAS STATION
That's right, it's a gas station. But this is no fast food McTacoSubwayBell. Located near the junction of Tioga Road and Highway 395 in Lee Vining, this otherwise nondescript mini-mart serves up a shockingly good selection of well-prepared meals. (Moderately priced, Brk-Lnch-Din, 760-647-1088)

MONO INN RESTAURANT
This pricey restaurant, located five miles north of Lee Vining, serves terrific food with fantastic views of Mono Lake. Reservations are recommended. Closed Tuesdays. (Expensive, Dinner only, 760-647-6581)

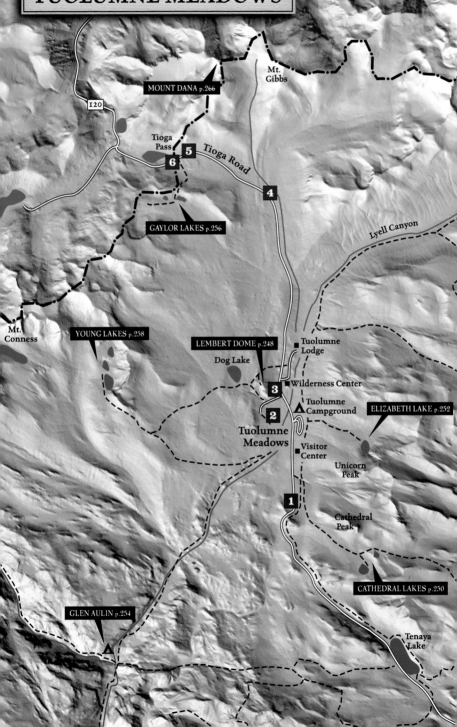

120

Mt.
Gibbs

MOUNT DANA p.266

Tioga
Pass

6 **5** Tioga Road

4

GAYLOR LAKES p.256

Lyell Canyon

Mt.
Conness

YOUNG LAKES p.258

LEMBERT DOME p.248

Dog Lake

Tuolumne
Lodge

3 Wilderness Center

Tuolumne
Campground

ELIZABETH LAKE p.252

2

Tuolumne
Meadows

Visitor
Center

Unicorn
Peak

1

Cathedral
Peak

CATHEDRAL LAKES p.250

GLEN AULIN p.254

Tenaya
Lake

1 Pothole Dome

A 200-foot scramble to the top of this small dome offers great views of Tuolumne Meadows. Pothole Dome is named for a series of rounded depressions (potholes) on its southern flank. The potholes are covered in a shiny rock that's often mistaken as glacial polish (a smooth veneer created when the underside of a moving glacier buffs the bedrock to a shine). But the polish on Pothole Dome's southern flank was created by water, not ice. During the Ice Age water flowed *under* a glacier that covered Pothole Dome. The water, channeled by a tunnel in the ice, flowed uphill over the dome, sculpting potholes and polishing the rock. Note: actual glacial polish can be seen on Pothole Dome's eastern slope.

2 Soda Spring/Parsons Lodge

This bubbling, naturally carbonated spring is hardly picturesque, but the views of Tuolumne Meadows and the surrounding peaks make it a worthy destination. The path to Soda Springs—an easy 1.5 mile stroll, perfect for visitors of all ages—starts from the Lembert Dome parking area. Follow the dirt road north and continue past the metal gate. After checking out Soda Spring, wander over to Parsons Lodge, a quaint stone lodge built by the Sierra Club in 1914. For decades Parsons Lodge was used as a Sierra Club meeting house. Today a handful of historic exhibits are featured inside, and free one-hour seminars are offered on weekend afternoons.

3 Lembert Dome

Lembert Dome, looming 900 feet over the eastern end of Tuolumne Meadows, is named for John-Baptiste Lembert, a sheepherder who homesteaded in Tuolumne Meadows in the late 1800s. How fitting, then, that the geological term used to describe the dome's shape is *roche moutonnée* (loose translation: stone sheep). Roche moutonnées form when glaciers flow over a large rock outcrop, smoothing out a gradual uphill slope and plucking away rocks as the glacier overrides the top to form a steep drop-off. A short trail heads to the top of Lembert Dome, which offers 360-degree views of Tuolumne Meadows and the surrounding peaks (p.248).

4 Mt. Dana/Mt. Gibbs View

This roadside pullout along the Dana Fork of the Tuolumne River offers great views of Mt. Dana and Mt. Gibbs. The pullout is marked by a small post labeled T36. At 13,053 feet Mt. Dana is the second highest peak in the park—only Mt. Lyell (13,114 feet) is taller. Mt. Gibbs (12,764 feet) is the fifth highest peak in the park. While savoring the view of Mt. Dana (on the left) and Mt. Gibbs, notice their dark coloration. The two peaks are composed of ancient metamorphic rocks that once covered all of Yosemite's granite. This is one of the few places in the park where the metamorphic rocks are still visible. A strenuous 3-mile hike heads to the top of Mt. Dana (p.266).

5 Dana Meadow

This beautiful meadow, located just west of the park boundary, lies 1,000 feet higher than Tuolumne Meadows. Twenty thousand years ago both meadows were buried under a massive glacier, but when global temperatures warmed around 15,000 years ago the ice started to melt. As the glacier retreated, huge chunks of ice broke off and formed depressions in the ground called kettles, which ultimately filled with water. The small ponds you see today are remnants of those kettles. You may also notice dozens of fallen trees on the north side of the meadow. The trees were knocked down several decades ago when an avalanche raced down the slopes above the meadow, which is why the fallen trees all point downhill.

6 Tioga Pass

At 9,941 feet, Tioga Pass is the highest paved road in California. It marks Yosemite's eastern boundary, which is also the watershed boundary for the Tuolumne River. (Precipitation that falls just west of Tioga Pass flows down the Tuolumne River toward the Central Valley, while precipitation that falls just east of Tioga Pass flows down Lee Vining Creek towards the Great Basin Desert.) As Highway 120 heads east from Tioga Pass, it plunges down the sheer eastern slope of the Sierra Nevada to the small town of Lee Vining. Along the way you'll be treated to great views of Tioga Lake, Ellery Lake, and Lee Vining Canyon.

⊰ LEMBERT DOME ⊱

SUMMARY   For a relatively quick Tuolumne hike with dramatic views, nothing beats Lembert Dome. Rising 9,450-feet over the east end of Tuolumne Meadows, Lembert Dome offers panoramic views of the High Sierra, including peaks along the eastern crest of the Sierra and the Cathedral Range. From the Dog Lake parking area the trail climbs through a forest, heads west at a junction, and emerges onto an open stretch of bare granite. At this point there's no official trail, but a series of cairns (small rock piles) will guide you towards the summit. With broad views of the western horizon, Lembert Dome is a fantastic spot to watch sunset (make sure to bring a flashlight or headlight for the hike down).

TRAILHEAD   The best (and shortest) route to the top of Lembert Dome starts from the Dog Lake parking area near Tuolumne Lodge. Take the free shuttle, or drive east on Tioga Road from Tuolumne Meadows and turn right towards Tuolumne Lodge. Follow the road to the Dog Lake parking area. The trail starts at the upper end of the parking area and crosses Tioga Road.

TRAIL INFO

RATING: Moderate

DISTANCE: 1.6 miles, round-trip

HIKING TIME: 1 hour

ELEVATION CHANGE: 850 feet

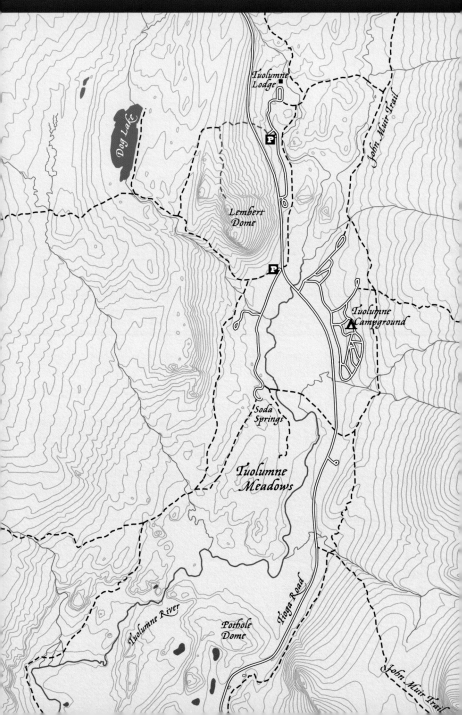

❧ CATHEDRAL LAKES ❧

SUMMARY These two small lakes, nestled along the John Muir Trail, are among the prettiest in Yosemite. Kick back on the smooth granite shores of Lower Cathedral Lake and soak in the dramatic views of Cathedral Peak, or continue to the flower-strewn meadows surrounding Upper Cathedral Lake and check out the peak from a different perspective. The hike to Cathedral Lakes is an uphill workout, but the scenery is definitely worth it. Lower Cathedral Lake, reached via a half-mile spur trail, is the larger of the two. If you've got a limited amount of time or energy, spend it here. But if your inner alpine lake lover is thirsting for more, continue one half mile past the spur trail to Upper Cathedral Lake. Backpacking note: Upper Cathedral Lake is a popular camping spot, but overnight camping is not allowed at Lower Cathedral Lake.

TRAILHEAD The trail to Cathedral Lakes starts about 1.5 miles west of the Tuolumne Visitor Center. Parking is often tight due to the trail's popularity, so consider riding the free shuttle from the Visitors Center.

TRAIL INFO

RATING: Moderate

HIKING TIME: 4–6 hours

DISTANCE: 7.5 miles, round-trip

ELEVATION CHANGE: 1,000 ft.

CATHEDRAL LAKES

⊰ ELIZABETH LAKE ⊱

SUMMARY While not as dramatic as Cathedral Lakes, Elizabeth Lake is a close runner up, with lush meadows and shimmering reflections of the granite peaks above. The round-trip hike is also three miles shorter—perfect for lake lovers with a limited amount of time. Once at Elizabeth Lake, check out Unicorn Peak towering above. The peak's "peculiar horn-shaped outline"—though hardly unicorn-esque from this angle—inspired the Whitney Survey to name it after the mythical creature. Experienced hikers can attempt a rugged scramble to the top of Unicorn Peak, which offers terrific 10,900-foot views of Tuolumne Meadows, but most visitors will be content to simply lounge around the lake. Following snowy winters a long snow chute often lingers at the far end of the lake. Note: camping is not allowed at Elizabeth Lake.

TRAILHEAD The trail to Elizabeth Lake starts in the Tuolumne Campground near the group camp restrooms on the B Loop. Signs in the campground will direct you to the trailhead. Don't be put off by the initial steep climb—the trail soon mellows out.

⊱ TRAIL INFO ⊰

RATING: Moderate   **HIKING TIME:** 3–4 hours

DISTANCE: 4.6 miles, round-trip   **ELEVATION CHANGE:** 850 feet

ELIZABETH LAKE

Lembert
Dome

Tioga Road

Tuolumne River

Tuolumne
Meadows

Visitor
Center

John Muir Trail

Tuolumne Campground

Unicorn Creek

Elizabeth
Lake

Unicorn
Peak

Johnson
Peak

✣ GLEN AULIN H.S.C. ✣

SUMMARY   Situated next to one of Yosemite's most spectacular backcountry waterfalls, Glen Aulin is many people's favorite High Sierra Camp. Even better: the hike to Glen Aulin from Tuolumne Meadows is almost entirely downhill, following the cascading Tuolumne River. You'll still have to hike uphill on the way back, but after a good night's rest in a comfy tent cabin you'll be ready to hit the trail. Glen Aulin is also the jumping off point for several long backpacks, including the Grand Canyon of the Tuolumne (p.276) and Matterhorn Canyon (p.280). Due to Glen Aulin's popularity, a backpackers campground with bear boxes and toilets is located behind the High Sierra Camp. (To protect the water quality of the Tuolumne drainage—San Francisco's water supply—Glen Aulin's high-tech composting toilet was built at a cost of several hundred thousand dollars—provoking some in the press to call it the "two-seat wonder.")

TRAILHEAD   From the Lembert Dome parking area, follow the broad path towards Soda Springs and then follow the signs to Glen Aulin.

◆ TRAIL INFO ◆

RATING: Moderate   **HIKING TIME:** 6–8 hours

DISTANCE: 10.4 miles, round-trip   **ELEVATION CHANGE:** 800 feet

～❧ GAYLOR LAKES ❧～

SUMMARY   This dramatic hike brings you to two shimmering lakes near the ruins of an old mining camp. Starting at an elevation of 10,000 feet, it's one of the highest day hikes in Yosemite—which means open scenery with terrific views of the surrounding High Sierra. The trail starts near the park's eastern boundary and immediately climbs steep a steep ridge with great views of Dana Meadow. From there the trail descends to the first lake, skirting the northern shore as the jagged peaks of the Cathedral Range seem to rise above the water to the west. Continue to the upper lake and you'll find permanent snowfields lying in the shade of the mountains. After wrapping around the shore, the trail climbs a small ridge that provides sweeping views of both lakes. Nearby are the crumbling remains of the Great Sierra Mine, a failed silver-mining operation that was established here in the 1800s. Note: camping is not allowed at Gaylor Lakes.

TRAILHEAD   The trail starts from the small parking area with a restroom just west of the Tioga Pass entrance station. You can also ride the free shuttle, which makes a handful of stops at Tioga Pass throughout the day during the summer.

◆ TRAIL INFO ◆

RATING: Moderate

HIKING TIME: 2–3 hours

DISTANCE: 5 miles, round-trip

ELEVATION CHANGE: 800 feet

❧ YOUNG LAKES ↢

SUMMARY These three picture-perfect lakes make a long, rewarding day hike or a terrific overnight backpack. Lower Young Lake, surrounded by lodge-pole pines and dramatic granite, is distinguished by its sandy beaches. Middle Young Lake is the smallest of the three, and Upper Young Lake, located above treeline, offers the most spectacular scenery. The shortest, most scenic route to Young Lakes heads towards Dog Lake and continues north. (Note: an alternate route, less steep but longer, branches off the Glen Aulin trail about a mile past Soda Springs.) If you're spending at least two nights at Young Lakes, nearby Mt. Conness makes a spectacular day hike—but only for rugged hikers who are used to off-trail travel. To climb Mt. Conness, head north from Middle or Upper Young Lake, skirt the ravine towards a series of marshy ponds, and pick up the unofficial use trail. Backpacking note: campfires are not allowed at Young Lakes.

TRAILHEAD The trailhead via Dog Lake starts near the picnic tables at the Lembert Dome parking area. The info listed below is for a hike to Lower Young Lake; Upper Young Lake is about 0.7 miles beyond Lower Young Lake

▸ TRAIL INFO ◂

RATING: Strenuous

DISTANCE: 13.5 miles, round-trip

HIKING TIME: 8–10 hours

ELEVATION CHANGE: 1,500 ft.

Roosevelt
Lake

Conness Lakes

Inyo
National
Forest

Conness Glacier

Mt.
Conness

Alpine
Lake

White
Mountain

Skelton
Lakes

Ragged
Peak

Young Lakes

Dog Lake

Tuolumne
Meadows

Lembert
Dome

Tioga Road

John Muir Trail

"The mighty Sierra, miles in height ... so gloriously
colored and so radiant, it seemed not clothed with
light but wholly composed of it, like the wall of
some celestial city .... Then it seemed to me that the
Sierra should be called, not the Nevada or Snowy
Range, but the Range of Light."

—John Muir

Mount Conness (left) from Young Lakes

Hiking between Young Lakes and Mt. Conness

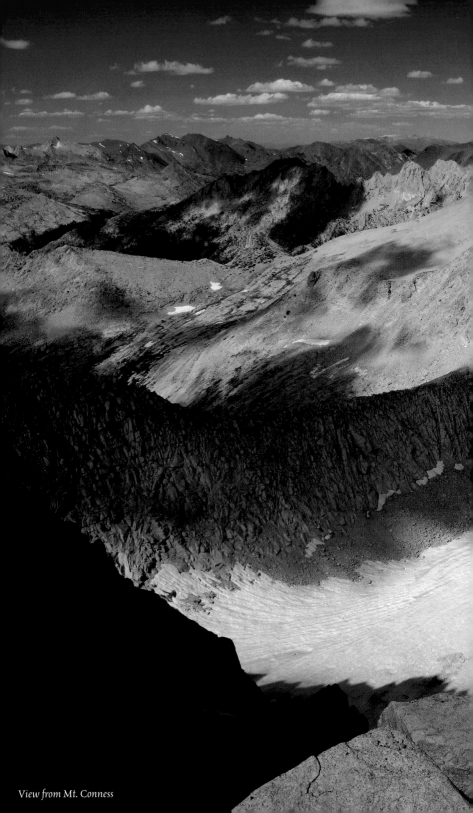

View from Mt. Conness

～⊰ MOUNT DANA ⊱～

SUMMARY At 13,053 feet, Mt. Dana is the second highest peak in the park; the highest, Mt. Lyell, is 13,114 feet. And while Mt. Lyell requires a rugged, multi-day backpack and technical climbing, Mt. Dana can be done in an afternoon. Perched on the eastern crest of the Sierra Nevada, you'll be treated to stunning, 360-degree views of the High Sierra, Mono Lake, and the eastern deserts. The unofficial—yet well-worn—trail to the top starts at the Tioga Pass Entrance Station and climbs 1,700 feet to an open ridge. The final 1,000 feet requires a scamper up scree (loose rocks). The final ascent can be confusing; stay near the eastern edge and look for cairns (small rock piles) to guide you. Note: Mt. Dana is often covered in snow well into the summer—ask about conditions before your hike. Note #2: if you see dark clouds approaching, do not attempt this hike.

TRAILHEAD The trail to Mt. Dana starts from the small parking area adjacent to the Tioga Pass Entrance Station. Ask the ranger at the kiosk for directions to the top, then follow the well-worn path east.

TRAIL INFO

RATING: Very Strenuous

DISTANCE: 5.8 miles, round-trip

HIKING TIME: 5–6 hours

ELEVATION CHANGE: 3,100 ft.

MOUNT DANA

Gardisky Lake

Tioga Peak

Lee Vining Canyon

Ellery Lake

Ansel Adams Wilderness

Tioga Lake

Inyo National Forest

Dana Plateau

Tioga Pass

Dana Lake

Dana Glacier

Mt. Dana

Dana Meadows

Yosemite National Park

Tioga Road

View from Mt. Dana

This alkaline lake, lying in the desert east of Yosemite, is famous for its unusual tufa towers: calcium carbonate spires (formed at underwater springs) that have recently been exposed due to low lake levels. Because Mono Lake has no outlet, dissolved salts from runoff concentrate over time. It's estimated that over 280 million tons of salt are dissolved in the lake, making it roughly 2.5 times as salty as the ocean.

In 1941 the city of Los Angeles extended its aqueduct system to divert water flowing into Mono Lake. Predictably, lake levels plummeted. The lake lost one-third of its surface area and Negit Island (previously in the center of the lake) turned into a peninsula. The island was a critical nesting site for birds—over 50,000 gulls, 85% of California's breeding population, nest at Mono Lake—and coyotes marched across the peninsula to feed on the bird's eggs. In 1978 the Mono Lake Committee teamed up with the Audubon Society to restore Mono Lake. In 1994 the lake's tributary streams won legal protection, and since then the lake's levels have been slowly rising.

In the depths of the Ice Age 20,000 years ago, Mono Lake was much larger than its present size. The surface of the ancient lake, called Lake Russell, lay at an elevation of about 7,140 feet—nearly 750 feet higher than today. Glaciers descending from the eastern slopes of the Sierra Nevada emptied directly into the lake, calving off icebergs into the water.

Mono Lake was named after the Mono Indians, who gathered alkali fly larvae along its shore. The larvae, called *kutsavi*, were crushed into a paste that was considered a delicacy. As one white explorer noted in 1863, "The Indians gave me some; it does not taste bad, and if one were ignorant of its origin, it would make fine soup."

Mono Lake from Mt. Dana

⨯ᐇ VOGELSANG H.S.C. ᐂ⨯

SUMMARY   At 10,100 feet, Vogelsang is the highest High Sierra Camp. While the other four High Sierra Camps are nestled among stately forests, Vogelsang is located above treeline, providing terrific views of the surrounding peaks. If you find yourself enthralled by Yosemite's granite landscapes, this is definitely the High Sierra Camp for you. In addition to grand views, there's a gurgling creek flowing through lush meadows—a great place to bask in the Sierra sunshine. And 500 feet above the High Sierra Camp is gorgeous Vogelsang Lake, nestled in a granite bowl between Vogelsang Peak (11,516) and Fletcher Peak (11,410). Backpackers heading to Vogelsang should seriously consider the 19-mile loop that passes Evelyn Lake and heads back to the trailhead via Lyell Canyon. The loop is one of the finest three-day backpacks in the park.

TRAILHEAD   The trail to Vogelsang starts from the parking area at Tuolumne Lodge. The lodge parking area is for guests only, so park in the nearby Dog Lake parking area or ride the free shuttle. Follow the John Muir Trail about a mile to Rafferty Creek, then heads towards Vogelsang.

◄ TRAIL INFO ►

RATING: Strenuous	**HIKING TIME:** 7–8 hours
DISTANCE: 13.6 miles, round-trip	**ELEVATION CHANGE:** 1,500 ft.

Vogelsang Lake

GRAND CANYON of the TUOLUMNE

SUMMARY This rugged backpack descends 4,700 feet down the stunning Grand Canyon of the Tuolumne River, then climbs 3,600 feet up to White Wolf Lodge. It's one of the most physically demanding backpacks in the park, but it's worth it. In places the Grand Canyon of the Tuolumne River rivals Arizona's Grand Canyon in depth. As you descend you'll be treated to dozens of roaring cascades, including the highlight of them all: Waterwheel Falls, where the river glides down a smooth granite slope, then explodes into a series of huge rooster-tail arcs. The trail continues below 5,000 feet in elevation, where black oaks and chaparral are common. Rattlesnakes are also present—keep your eyes out. Spend the night in Pate Valley and rest up for the next day's grueling ascent. After reaching White Wolf, you'll be ready for a hot shower and a cozy bed. Book a night at White Wolf Lodge before your trip and finish off the hike in style.

TRAILHEAD Hike down to Glen Aulin (p.254) from Tuolumne Meadows. From Glen Aulin continue following the Tuolumne River downhill.

TRAIL INFO

RATING: Very Strenuous   **HIKING TIME:** 2–3 days

DISTANCE: 28 miles, one-way   **ELEVATION CHANGE:** 4,700 ft.

GRAND CANYON
OF THE TUOLUMNE

Tuolumne
Meadows

Glen Aulin
H.S.C.

Sunrise
H.S.C.

Waterwheel
Falls

Tenaya
Lake

May Lake
H.S.C.

Ten Lakes

Muir
Gorge

Porcupine
Flat

Tioga Road

Pate
Valley

Yosemite
Creek

White
Wolf

Hetch Hetchy
Reservoir

"For miles the river is one wild, exulting, on-rushing mass ... gliding in magnificent silver plumes, dashing and foaming through huge boulder-dams, leaping high into the air in wheel-like whirls ... singing in exuberance of mountain energy."

—John Muir

Waterwheel Falls

❧ MATTERHORN CANYON ❧

SUMMARY   Lying in the remote northeast corner of the park, Matterhorn Canyon is one of the most spectacular and seldom visited locations in Yosemite. Getting here requires several days of backpacking through rugged wilderness, but for quintessential High Sierra beauty—snow-capped granite peaks, flowery meadows, glacially carved U-shaped valleys—few hikes in the Sierra Nevada can compare. After following the Pacific Crest Trail for 20 miles from Tuolumne Meadows, you'll head north into Matterhorn Canyon. The jagged Sawtooth Range looms above as you march up to Burro Pass (10,600). After savoring the dramatic views, drop down into the meadowy, boulder-strewn canyon that heads to Mule Pass (10,400). Say goodbye to Yosemite as you enter the Hoover Wilderness, which treats you to a handful of idyllic lakes before the hike ends at bustling, touristy Twin Lakes.

TRAILHEAD   From Tuolumne Meadows head to Glen Aulin (p.254), then follow the Pacific Crest Trail through Cold Canyon. Note: this one-way trip ends at Twin Lakes, where you can leave your car for several days for a small fee.

TRAIL INFO

RATING: Very Strenuous   **HIKING TIME:** 6–8 days

DISTANCE: 38.4 miles, round-trip   **ELEVATION CHANGE:** 3,500 ft.

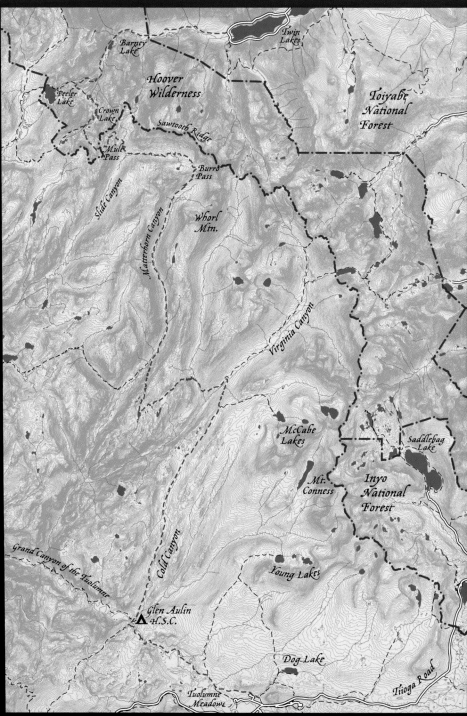

Matterhorn Canyon

Sawtooth Range from Mule Pass

WAWONA

THIS area, the southernmost tip of Yosemite, is unremarkable compared to the rest of the park. There's little in the way of dramatic scenery—no sheer cliffs or thousand-foot waterfalls—just a lazy meadow rolling through the forest. Still, Wawona is noteworthy for three popular attractions: the Mariposa Grove of giant sequoias, the Wawona Hotel, and the Pioneer History Center.

The Mariposa Grove, located just east of the park's South Entrance Station, is justly famous as the largest grove of giant sequoias in the park. Among its 500 plus specimens is Grizzly Giant, the largest tree in the park. About six miles northwest of the Mariposa Grove you'll find the Wawona Hotel and the Pioneer History Center. Adjacent to the Hotel is the Wawona Information Center (209-375-9531), a small building where a knowledgeable staff answers questions, issues wilderness permits, and sells a large collection of books and maps. Just north of the hotel is the Wawona Store, which sells groceries and other basics. A post office and gas station (24-hour credit card payment accepted) are also located nearby. There's no gas in Yosemite Valley—25 miles distant, about an hour's drive—so it's a good idea to fill up here. Continue along Wawona Road and you'll soon pass Wawona Campground, where free ranger-led campfire programs are often held at night. Nature walks and other programs are also offered (check *Yosemite Today* for seasonal times and dates).

For hundreds of years local Indians lived near present-day Wawona along the banks of the South Fork of the Merced River. They referred to the area as *Pallachun* ("Good Place to Stop"). In the fall, when the river ran low, the Indians dumped large quantities of crushed soaproot into the water. According to Galen Clark, who moved to the area in 1856 (p.102), the soaproot "roiled the water and made it somewhat foamy. The fish were soon affected by it, became stupid with a sort of strangulation, and rose to the surface, where they were easily captured by the Indians with their scoop baskets."

Shortly after moving here, Clark opened a small hotel catering to tourists on their way to Yosemite Valley. It was said that of all the supplies delivered to Clark's Station, cases of wine, whiskey, and brandy far outnumbered cases of food. Clark was a popular host, but a lousy businessman, and in 1874 he sold his hotel to the Washburn brothers. In 1879 they built the Wawona Hotel, and in 1882 they renamed the area *Wah-wo-nah*, the supposed local Indian name for giant sequoias. It's claimed that the word is an imitation of a hooting owl, considered the guardian spirit of the Big Trees.

Left: Wawona Hotel

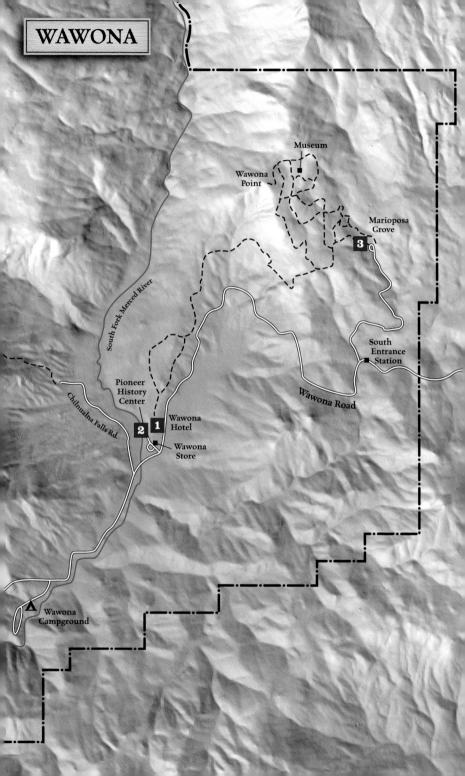

WAWONA

Museum

Wawona Point

Marioposa Grove

3

South Fork Merced River

South Entrance Station

Wawona Road

Pioneer History Center

Chilnualna Falls Rd.

2 **1** Wawona Hotel

Wawona Store

Wawona Campground

1 Wawona Hotel

This beautiful hotel, built in 1879, is full of 19th century Victorian charm. In 1888 a popular guidebook depicted the Wawona Hotel with a dramatic fountain in front—despite the fact that no fountain existed. So many guests complained about the missing fountain that the owners installed one, and it continues to greet visitors to this day. Even if you're not a guest, the elegant dining room serves great upscale cuisine (209-375-1425), and local celebrity Tom Bopp frequently plays piano in the lobby/lounge. Saturday BBQs on the lawn are another summer treat, and evening cocktails on the front porch never fail to please. If you'd like to check out the hotel's nine-hole golf course, stop by the Wawona Golf Shop (209-375-6572), which offers rentals and organizes tee times.

2 Pioneer History Center

This small cluster of historic buildings, relocated here in the 1960s from other parts of the park, is just beyond the Wawona Store. There are cabins, a jail, a Wells Fargo office, a blacksmith shop, a collection of vintage stagecoaches and (for those who prefer the real thing) genuine horse-drawn stage rides. The ten minute ride costs a few dollars per person. Walk across the covered bridge—one of only a half dozen in California—to the main square and look for posted signs listing dates and times for stage rides and other activities, including campfires and weekend barn dances.

Grizzly Giant

3 Mariposa Grove

Over 500 giant sequoias are scattered throughout this impressive 250-acre grove. You can drive to the Mariposa Grove, but the adjacent parking lot fills up quickly in the summer. A better option is the free daily shuttle that makes stops at Wawona Store, South Entrance, and Mariposa Grove (9am–6pm, May–Oct). Hiking trails crisscross the grove, and narrated tram tours depart daily from the parking area every 20 minutes. Tickets cost about $10. If you'd rather hike, venture at least 0.8 miles to Grizzly Giant. Or, if you're feeling energetic, huff and puff up to the quaint Mariposa Grove Museum (above), where you'll find fascinating exhibits about the Big Trees inside.

There are many gargantuan trees in the grove, but the 2,700 year old Grizzly Giant tops the list. Over 20 stories high with a base 96 feet around, it's the larg-est giant sequoia in Yosemite and the fifth largest organism on the planet. One of its branches is six feet in diameter—larger than the trunks of most full-grown trees in the park. The nearby California Tree has a tunnel that was cut through the trunk in 1895. (For more on giant sequoias, see p.68.)

HETCH HETCHY

LOCATED ROUGHLY 12 miles northeast of the park's Big Oak Flat Entrance—40 driving miles from Yosemite Valley—Hetch Hetchy is definitely off the beaten path. If you're visiting Yosemite for the first time, spend your time elsewhere. But if you're fascinated by the reservoir's tumultuous history, Hetch Hetchy and its springtime waterfalls are worth a look.

Today Hetch Hetchy is an 8-mile long, 117 billion gallon reservoir. Each day 220 million gallons of Hetch Hetchy water are delivered to 2.4 million consumers in the San Francisco Bay Area. The water, which flows downhill along a 167-mile aqueduct, is so pure that it's usually exempted from federal water filtration requirements. And hydropower from O'Shaughnessy Dam generates 1.7 *billion* kilowatt-hours annually—enough to power 325,000 Bay Area households.

Before the dam was completed in 1923, Hetch Hetchy was a beautiful valley that was, in many ways, comparable to Yosemite. The first white man to set eyes on Hetch Hetchy was Nathan Screech, who arrived in the 1850s. Screech encountered several Indians cooking a plant called *hatchhatchie*, and the word, later anglicized to "Hetch Hetchy," became the name of the valley.

When San Francisco politicians proposed flooding Hetch Hetchy in the early 1900s, John Muir and the Sierra Club fought back, but their efforts were ultimately defeated in a contentious legal battle (p.112). In 1987 Secretary of the Interior Donald Hodel suggested tearing down the dam and restoring Hetch Hetchy Valley. Hodel's suggestion, which was vehemently opposed by several prominent California politicians, ultimately went nowhere. In 1999 the nonprofit group Restore Hetch Hetchy was founded, and in 2006 California's Department of Water Resources released a report that found "no fatal flaws in the restoration concept that would preclude additional study." Cost estimates of removing the dam range anywhere from one to ten billion dollars.

Hetch Hetchy is only open during daylight hours. To get there, exit Yosemite via the Big Oak Flat Entrance, drive one mile, and turn right onto Evergreen Road. Continue roughly seven miles to Mather Campground, then turn right towards the Hetch Hetchy Entrance Station. From the entrance it's about eight miles to Hetch Hetchy. There's a parking area next to the dam, and an easy 2.5 mile trail skirts the reservoir's northern shore en route to Tueeulala and Wapama Falls. The trail starts at the large tunnel next to the dam.

Left: Tueelulala and Wapama Falls

Ahwahnee Dining Room 129
Ahwahnee Hotel 36, 162
Ansel Adams Gallery 134
Backpacking 19
Badger Pass Ski Area 191
Bear Canisters 22
Bears 34
Belding's Ground Squirrel 70
Bighorn Sheep 72
Biking 129
Black Bear 74
Bracebridge Dinner 131
Bridalveil Creek Campground 38
Bridalveil Fall 150
Camp 4 37, 138
Camping 36
Cathedral Beach 152
Cathedral Lakes 250
Chefs' Holidays 131
Clark Range 206
Clark Range View 191
Clouds Rest 230
Cocktails 130
Coyote 76
Crane Flat Campground 38
Curry Village 36, 129, 157
Dana Meadow 247
Degnan's Deli 129
Degnan's Pizza Loft 130
Devils Elbow 138
Dining 129, 243
Ecology 57
El Capitan 140
Elizabeth Lake 252
El Portal 39
Entrance Fees 32
Fish Camp 39
Four Mile Trail 178

Gas 33
Gaylor Lakes 256
Geology 41
Giant Sequoia 68
Glacier Point 194
Glacier Point Road 189
Glen Aulin 254
Grand Canyon, Tuolumne 276
Groceries 130
Groveland 39
Half Dome 158, 172
Happy Isles 160
Hetch Hetchy 293
High Sierra Camps 27
Hiking 19
Hiking, Best Hikes 23
Horseback Rides 243
Hodgdon Meadow Campground 38
Hotels 36
Housekeeping Camp 36
Information 33
Introduction 9
LeConte Memorial 154
Lee Vining 39
Lembert Dome 246, 248
Lodging 36
Lower Pines Campground 37
Lyell Glacier 54
Mariposa 39
Mariposa Grove 291
Marmot 86
Matterhorn Canyon 280
May Lake 228
Midpines 39
Mirror Lake 160
Mist Trail 166
Mono Lake 270
Mountain Lion 78

Mountain Room 130
Mt. Conness 258
Mt. Dana 246, 266
Mt. Gibbs 246
Mule Deer 80
North Dome 224
North Pines Campground 37
Oakhurst 39
Olmstead Point 218
Outdoor Gear 131
Parsons Lodge 245
Peregrine Falcon 82
Permits, Wilderness 20
Pioneer History Center 289
Pohono Trail 202
Porcupine Flat Campground 38
Post Office 134
Pothole Dome 245
Rafting 31
Restaurants 129, 243
Rock Climbing 25
Rockfalls 160
Sentinel Beach 152
Sentinel Dome 200
Sentinel Falls 154
Shuttle 32
Sierra Nevada 53
Skiing 30
Soda Spring 245
Steller's Jay 84
Sunrise 234
Taft Point 198
Tamarack Flat Campground 38
Tenaya Lake 223
Ten Lakes 236
Tioga Pass 247
Tioga Road 215
Trees 62

Tunnel View 146
Tuolumne Grove 218
Tuolumne Meadows 241
Tuolumne Meadows Campground 37
Tuolumne Meadows Lodge 37
Upper Pines Campground 37
Village Grill 130
Vintners' Holidays 131
Vogelsang 272
Washburn Point 191
Waterwheel Falls 278
Wawona 287
Wawona Campground 38
Wawona Hotel 38, 289
Weather 21
White Wolf Campground 38
White Wolf Lodge 38
Wilderness Centers 20
Wildflowers 64
YARTS 32
Yosemite Association 131
Yosemite Cemetery 134
Yosemite Chapel 154
Yosemite Creek Campground 38
Yosemite Falls 134, 180
Yosemite Indian Village 134
Yosemite Lodge 36
Yosemite Museum 134
Yosemite Valley 127
Yosemite Village 134
Yosemite Visitor Center 134
Young Lakes 258

The Best of the Best

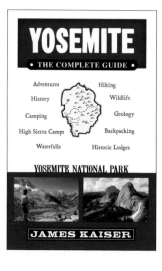

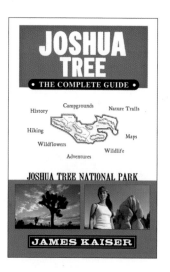

www.jameskaiser.com